Going Down for Gum Wrappers

Going Down for Gum Wrappers

Bob Lancaster

L. R. ARK.

August House / Little Rock
P U B L I S H E R S

Printed in the United States of America

First edition 1986

10 9 8 7 6 5 4 3 2 1

Library of Congress Cataloging-in-Publication Data:

Lancaster, Bob.
Going down for gum wrappers.
1. Lancaster, Bob - Biography.
2. Authors, American - 20th century - Biography.
I. Title.
PS3562.A4667Z466   1986   818'.5409 [B]   86-70038
ISBN 0-87483-009-5 (pbk.)

Some of the experiences recounted here were first described
or mentioned in the *Pine Bluff Commercial*, the *Arkansas Democrat*, the *Arkansas Gazette*, the *Harvard Crimson*, the *Philadelphia
Inquirer*, *Arkansan* magazine, and the *Arkansas Times* magazine.

This book is dedicated to the memory of Joe D. Lancaster.

INTRODUCTORY NOTE

This is a peculiar work — a memoir written in the third person. There's no explaining the approach; it's just a mystery, like the way cats look at you, or the song "The Duke of Earl." The events recounted here are true, and nearly all the people are real people. I left most of them with their real names, even when those names weren't particularly mellifluous or apt. I changed a few of them for good reasons, one of which was residual physical fear. Some of the people here may remember these incidents differently, but that's the way it goes. I aimed to tell the truth, but this is not history, it's a meditation on the elusiveness of identity, and some minor embellishments might have survived my conscientious attempts to purge them. I apologize for a few fugitive instances also of literary license: for example, the bottle with the note in it was a metaphorical bottle — a way of making a long story shorter. But otherwise, the book is one hundred per cent accurate and truthful. Or ninety-seven per cent, at the very least.

A word about the title: "Going down for gum wrappers" is a description that I heard an old rassler use to describe the rewards that come to those who face the perils and indignities of the rassling ring until they are too old, fat, hurt, or humili- ated to go on. I'm sorry I don't remember this old warrior's name. I recall only that he was from Florida, weighed in excess of four hundred pounds, and, for some sensible reason that I have also forgotten, named the actor Walter Pidgeon as the person he most admired.

BL

CHAPTER ONE

Bruiser Pursued

Bruiser sounds like a name for a heavy, not a hero. The name of some big old Ajax or Baby Huey — a Kong-got-aloose, strewing pumpknots and shiners with a mindless and lumbering prodigiality. Bruiser was nothing like that, but he tried to be philosophical about the name. "It could be worse," he said. "I've known people who came to be called Buttbreath and Fishface. By their *friends.* I was always glad I wasn't my town's designated Dub. Every little town I knew had a designated Dub. Nothing against it, but I just can't imagine somebody named Dub ever probing very deeply into the mysteries of human identity, you know what I mean?"

It should be noted that Bruiser had nothing to do with selecting the name. It was put on him, like one of those *Kick Me* signs that pranksters stick on the back of your shirt, by a blind man during Bruiser's days as a professional wrestler, or rassler. Bruiser was an earnest young man of twenty-five at that time, and already well along into a career as a journalist. It had never entered his mind to throw over his position as resident laffs columnist for a gloomy old Little Rock newspaper called the *Arkansas Democrat* in order to turn rassler. If someone had told him he had to die or become a professional rassler — or have both knees smashed with a sledgehammer or become a professional rassler — he might have considered it. Otherwise, no.

And yet it came to pass, at least in that paradoxical, dualistic sense that was always waylaying Bruiser. And it left him with the name.

Little Rock, Arkansas, at that time was a weekly stop on the circuit of a "championship" rassling troupe out of Tulsa, Oklahoma. Tulsa had also produced Anita Bryant and Oral Roberts, so it didn't feel guilty about regularly loosing this sty of rasslers on neighboring states and cities, even those that had never done it any harm. Every Tuesday night, the Tulsa rasslers came to Little Rock to grapple sweatily for a couple of hours in the basement of Joe T. Robinson Auditorium, named for Joe T. Robinson, the 1928 Democratic vice-presidential nominee. Several hundred easily entertained Arkansas people paid money to see them. Not Bruiser. The matches were delayed-telecast the following Saturday morning and easily entertained Arkansas people who hadn't got to see them in person got to see them then. Not Bruiser.

Bruiser was a thoughtful, artistic person looking to find his true identity, his destiny, in some noble realm and expecting to find it any day, so he couldn't be going to rassling matches or watching them on TV. He used the time instead to do things like read the letters of Pliny the Younger and practice his wine tasting. Both of these activities tended to induce in him an unbecoming drowsiness, but the effort was sincere and his disdain for rassling and its mob was genuine. So he and Championship Professional Wrestling of Tulsa, Oklahoma, might never the twain have met had it not been for the relentless matchmaking of Bruiser's son, Bruiser Jr.

Bruiser Jr. was six years old. He no longer believed in Santy but he still believed in professional rassling. He never missed those Saturday morning telecasts. He rooted for the heroes and hissed the villains with honest enthusiasm. He raved about dirty tactics and referee incompetence. His dream was to be a spectator at ringside — to attend a Tuesday night bout at the auditorium and see some of the legendary lummoxes in the flab.

Bruiser tried to put him off by taking him to baseball games and the Roller Derby. He took him bowling and miniature golfing, and played Rook and Chinese checkers with him, and always let him win except for a few times to keep up his own morale. But he ran out of excuses finally, and he and Bruiser Jr. spent a grotesque Tuesday evening with the Tulsa gladiators and their Boetian admirers.

Bruiser Jr. wasn't disappointed. The spectacle of grown men twisting and pawing and flopping around on one another was, he said, the funnest experience of his life.

His father composed an obligatory description of the events of the evening and this was routinely published in the newspaper. Bruiser had no desire to destroy his little boy's illusions about the "sport" so he made only subtle between-the-lines implications that "professional" "wrestling" was a freak show for the amusement of the unwashed. He never imagined that this charitable account might offend anyone, but it did. Loyal rassling fans wrote letters (well, they tried) and some even called at the *Democrat* newsroom, ready to rumble and threatening to do step-over-toeholds on Bruiser's private parts. A large rawboned woman who called herself Murtha came in and snatched Bruiser up by the shirt collar and told him she was going to wring his scrawny neck. Bruiser knew she meant it, too. Murtha was a sporting-life legend in Little Rock. Her pastime was whipping the rassling crown into a bloodthirst. More than once, when a thug had cheated out a decision over a Tarzan-looking crowd favorite, Murtha had stormed into the ring and mugged the referee. She was also a fixture at the Arkansas Travelers minor league baseball games, sitting in a box seat along the first base line, peppering the first-base ump with sharp-edged pebbles which she blew through a soda straw. Bruiser had no desire to tangle with this aurochs, so when she snatched him up there in the newsroom, he cravenly promised to write a retraction.

He felt no obligation to keep that promise, though, having made it under duress. So once Murtha was gone, he authored an article telling her and the rassling establishment what he really thought of them. He told them they were as crazy as they looked if they thought they could destroy the First Amendment by sending one of their goons to intimidate an honest reporter. They weren't living in Russia, he reminded them. This was the USA, where a man could speak his mind without fear of reprisal except from the Mafia or the Klan or the FBI or the House UnAmerican Activities Committee or a nut with a gun. He wrote with righteous fury, with patriotic heat. When he finished the article, he congratulated himself on it and solicited plaudits from colleagues, one of whom, the sports editor, called it "the most vigorous indictment of the negligible that I have seen." He sagely suggested that Bruiser slip it into the trash can. Bruiser pondered this good advice and uncharacteristically took it.

But there's a rule in the writing business which holds that one's scribbles are likely to see print in inverse proportion to one's desire to see them in print: your masterpiece may languish, but ink some unpardonable scrawl and it will find publication, conquering all obstacles and defying the odds, and will likely endure to become your epitaph. A harsh truth, and sure enough, when Bruiser opened the newspaper the next day he beheld his rassling manifesto nailed there with Lutherian defiance on the front page. What word would best describe his reaction? — Woebegone? Simpering? Hysterical? Murtha had hurt people for looking at her wrong. What might she do to someone who had called her a *goon*?

Bruiser was enormously relieved when the promoter for the rassling troupe rang up and sounded friendly. This was the blind man. His name was McGuirk. He wanted to come by the newsroom for an amicable powwow, he said, and he would be glad to intercede in Bruiser's behalf with possibly overzealous fans like Murtha. During the powwow, he said he had heard that Murtha was really steamed, all right, but he said he would personally ask her to lay off. He invited Bruiser to return to the auditorium the following Tuesday night to see the matches at ringside as his special guest. He gave Bruiser a complimentary ticket.

His congeniality made Bruiser suspicious, and Bruiser told him so.

McGuirk confessed, then, that he wanted to give the fans a chance to boo Bruiser and throw a few beer bottles at him and such. It would be good advertising for them both, he said.

"I won't do it," Bruiser told him. "I don't care if you *are* blind."

"Okay, pal, who needs you then?" McGuirk said ominously. He arose in what Bruiser interpreted to be a sudden huff and stalked out of the room. Bruiser had never before seen a blind person stalk, but that was how he described the grim purposeful way that McGuirk took his departure. He *stalked.*

Bruiser stayed home the next few days, with the drapes closed. He wouldn't go to work because he was convinced that Murtha was going to jump out at him with a meat cleaver. The few times he left the house, he asked his wife Scamp to start the car for him, but she wouldn't do it. He stayed away from work until the following Tuesday, and when he sneaked back to the office then he found an official-looking envelope in his mailbox. Inside was a letter informing him that he had been duly licensed to wrestle professionally in the state of Arkansas. It was signed by the chairman of the Arkansas Athletic Commission. Bruiser checked it out and found that the license was legitimate. Also, in the sports section of that day's newspaper was an advertisement announcing the main event on the wrestling card that evening at the auditorium. The headline on the ad said:

SURPRISE OPPONENT vs. BOB LANCASTER

Bruiser felt a Hitchcockian chill: "Bob Lancaster" was the name he went by at the time. What was the blind man up to?

Bruiser *had* to attend, of course. He went incognito, with a hat pulled low on his brow and a trenchcoat high on the scruff of his neck. He found a nose-and-glasses disguise in Bruiser Jr.'s toy box and took it along to slip on in case he got seated close to Murtha. He shouldered anonymously into the large, surly crowd entering the auditorium, and got to his seat inconspicuously. So far, so good.

And the rassling started out as routine Tulsa-style Joe T. Robinson Auditorium fare. A masked tag team gored up the ring with their opponents, a pair of Dudley Dorights from Canada. Then a Ugandan midget won by default over a dwarf Turk, who gave up after the former, using the "pygmy face claw," inadvertently gouged out the latter's left eye. Or that's what the Turk claimed, anyway. As the Turk staggered away toward the dressing room, a granny-looking old lady sitting beside Bruiser yelled, "Get back in that ring, you chickenshit!"

A while later an Oriental giant defeated a black bear, and as the bear was led out of the ring, McGuirk, in his opaque glasses, was led in. He got a standing ovation while he groped around for the overhead microphone. Then, with much theatrical disgust and contempt, he recited some of Bruiser's newspaper allegations about how this beloved corps of first-rate world-class wrestlers were just a bunch of big fat Tulsa phonies.

All around Bruiser, the fans booed and screamed for this scoundrel Lancaster's blood. Bruiser screamed and booed with them, not wanting to give himself away.

"Lies! Infamy!" McGuirk shouted, and the spectators roared their agreement.

"Wouldn't you just love to have the so-and-so here and watch the boys tie him in knots and *feed* him a few of these sorry lies?" the blind man said.

The crowd erupted again, and Bruiser as rabidly as anyone.

"Well, as a matter of fact, he *is* here!" McGuirk shouted triumphantly.

Bruiser shrank down in his seat, expecting the glare of a spotlight to fall upon him directly, and then the savage pack.

But the spotlight and the attention moved *away* from him, and he slumped with relief as the crowd craned to watch two uniformed security guards dragging a grotesque and forlorn creature down the middle aisle toward the ring. This character was indescribably gross, bald and beady-eyed, with a sunken chest and a mammoth butt and spindly little knobby-kneed legs. He was dressed in pink tights, and he was pleading theatrically with the guards not to make him enter the ring.

The blind man introduced him as Bruiser Bob Lancaster, and the crowd booed and spat and threw things for what must have been five minutes. Then McGuirk called for quiet and announced that this whimpering mass of tallow would wrestle not one but *all* the upstanding athletes he had defamed. Bruiser Bob got down on his knees and implored the blind man, but McGuirk just kicked him away.

Bruiser Bob's first "opponent" was the popular golden-haired "World Junior Middleweight Champion," who didn't even give him a chance to whine before flattening him with a flying dropkick. The crowd laughed and hooted while Bruiser Bob lay writhing and groaning. The "champ" then gave way to the Mad Dog Brothers, the masked pair who had eviscerated the Dorights earlier, and they tortured Bruiser Bob with some ear-twists and Apache finger-spreads. Then one of them lifted him in a reverse full Nelson while the other pulled down the pink tights to reveal BB's canyonesque posterior cleavage. The crowd cheered and whistled appreciatively.

Out in the bleachers, the real Bruiser nudged the old lady sitting beside him and said sardonically, "Only in America."

"Goddam right!" she said, clapping and whistling madly.

The Mad Dogs willed Bruiser Bob to the Dorights, who, still dripping catsup, were content to bodyslam him for a while, much to the crowd's disappointment. The Ugandan and the Turk (who had meantime covered his empty socket with an eyepatch) whaled away on the Bruiser blubber for a time, then each grabbed an arm and heaved him over the ropes, smashing the broadcasters' table with him and leaving him bloodied and broken on the arena floor.

Bruiser Bob staggered to his feet and retreated, with piteous cries, down the aisle toward the dressing room, pelted by missiles hurled by fans and chased by the other rasslers, including the bear, who hadn't yet got their licks in.

Murtha joined the pack, taking roundhouse swipes at him with her purse.

Bruiser Jr. watched this fiasco on the delayed telecast the following Saturday. He was embarrassed, and denounced Bruiser for not having put up a better fight.

"But that wasn't *me*, son," Bruiser protested. "That guy was an imposter. He didn't even *look* like me."

"I'll never be able to show my face in this town again," the boy said, unconsoled.

Bruiser spent the ensuing weeks and months trying to live down the name that had been albatrossed onto him by a blind man who was nothing like Homer or Tiresias or Milton or Ray Charles. But the name wouldn't go away. Years later he was still getting letters that began with the salutation:

Dear Bruiser (ha ha):

These weren't just from dimwitted rassling fans either. They were from important people — congressmen, advertising men, TV weathermen, and the like. But Bruiser reconciled himself to the name in time. It wasn't the name of somebody who was going to amount to much: it wasn't Hemingway or Bogie or Lindy or Elvis or Wolfgang. But it was a name that was apt, somehow. *Bruiser.* Aye, life is full of bruises. Bruises on one's shins, bruises on one's ego, bruises on one's dreams. In the sense of receiving rather than dispensing life's contusions, a bruiser was what Bruiser certainly was.

CHAPTER TWO

A Small Uncertainty Flutters By

Long before Bruiser became Bruiser, he was the sixth of seven children growing up in a peasant family in the pine-and-honeysuckle country just outside a small town in a rural region of a southern state. The state was Arkansas and the town was Sheridan. Arkansas was one of the states of the Old Confederacy, and Sheridan was named for Phil Sheridan, the mongoloid Union general. Sheridan was a vicious man who hated the South as much as he hated Indians, and naming an Arkansas town for him was a scalawag legislature's idea of a Reconstruction joke. The town of Sheridan was in Grant County. More of the same joke.

Bruiser didn't know about this old insult when he was growing up, but he wouldn't have cared about it if he had known. He didn't have much of a sense of history. He knew that Jesus had been crucified around two thousand years before, and that God had created the heavens and the earth some time before that. Other than that, he was willing to let bygones be bygones.

Five of his brothers and sisters were at least seven years older than Bruiser, and the eldest, his brother Harold, was in the Navy chasing Japanese submarines in the South Pacific when Bruiser was born. His brother Bill was three years younger than Bruiser, though, and Bruiser always thought of him as just a little kid, even after they both got old enough to be grampas. So Bruiser felt alone in the middle much of the time. Trying to straddle the void between the wise old heads and the brat. He wasn't unhappy or maladjusted or psychotic about this, just vaguely unsure of what this duality demanded of him — just ever so slightly disturbed at having this tiny element of uncertainty fluttering around his life.

Arkansas was a farming state and Sheridan had once been a farming community, but it had been a sawmill town since twenty years before Bruiser was born. Harvesting trees rather than cotton. Bruiser's wasn't a farming family but it wasn't exactly a notfarming family either. They sometimes had a cow, always a few chickens scratching around in the back yard, usually a vegetable garden with onions, radishes, beets, red potatoes, snap beans, okra, purple-hull peas and tomatoes; but there was none of the bucolic chopping-cotton-builds-character farmlife that Bruiser would later describe with great fraudulent nostalgia to his children. He also would regale them with an ever more elaborate tale of boyhood hours spent in the hot sun plowing behind a white mule, and while this wasn't exactly a lie, it was certainly a gigantic magnification. When he was seven or eight years old, he did indeed rashly volunteer to plow a row in the garden. He didn't give up the attempt until after he'd had time to discover that Mr. West's borrowed mule could be enormously flatulent as well as contrary, and would, if it took a mind to, make a dash for open country, dragging in tow through nettle and stinkweed shouting miniature ploughman Bruiser, along with a length of garden fence, a trailing creeper of bluebells, and an impressive accumulation of vegetable, animal and mineral field debris. About two minutes of husbandry for Bruiser and that was that.

Bruiser's father had been a farmer as a young man but had gone over to sawmilling when Sheridan did. He was a night-shift sawmill worker who spent his daylight waking hours doing odd jobs around Sheridan — roofing and painting houses, laying concrete, fixing things. So while Bruiser counted himself as a country child, he was more of a Turgenev or Flaubert country child than a Faulkner one: he never had hookworm disease or had to go without shoes, and he wasn't slackjawed or inbred or dumb. His family home, a thrown-together plank house beside a dirt road, wasn't symbolic like Tara or Uncle Tom's cabin: it wasn't haunted either; it was staple country shelter, with a well and a butane tank and a front porch and a shed full of junk and scorpions and lizards, and it just happened to squat in the exact center of the ptolemaic Little Bruiser universe.

That universe was the most interesting one Bruiser would inhabit. By day, it had meadows where wars raged against Japs and Comanches and wolves and gangsters and icky Plutonians, and where, during the truces, pennants and Olympic medals and Indianapolis 500s were won. It had wild plum orchards, and sweetgum trees that had more personality than any of Bruiser's aunts. It had buried conquistador treasure and a magic creek with no source and no mouth, and Tarzan grapevines and crawfish castles that squished mud up between Bruiser's toes when he stepped on them. Rabbits and blue racers lived only for Bruiser to chase, and grasshoppers for him to bait fishhooks with, and butterflies for him to see again when he closed his eyes in bed at night, and dandelion tops for him to blow. Arrowheads littered the home place only so he could pick them up, put them in his pocket, and damage the wringer on his mother's new washing machine with them. Clouds were sailing ships, and the original gods, evident to Bruiser as to most children, played timeless in the innocent blue Bruiser sky. By night the Bruiser universe was filled with other gods who strode the air — Red Ryder and The Shadow; and when the nights were warm and scuppernong, Little Bruiser's mother, or one of his older sisters, Nita or Joy or Bet, would swing him to sleep in the front-porch swing, called to by whippoorwills, shivered by owls, and then would carry him quietly back inside and put him to bed. He possumed sometimes when they carried him, as limp and languid as an old cat.

Except for that little element of uncertainty fluttering by, all was just that sweet and indulgent. Little Bruiser was not suspicious of the future, and he appeared as snug in the scheme of homeplace life as Adam in early Eden.

Little League baseball came to Sheridan when Bruiser was ten years old. It was the grandest experience for him since electricity had come to the home place when he was six; and it must have been the most exciting development in Sheridan since Bill & Elsie's Cafe had put up its three-color neon sign, pink and yellow and green, which people drove all the way from Grapevine and Poyen and Leola just to behold.

Awesome light towers reared one day over a sandy corner of the old schoolyard, and unbelievably generous merchant sponsors put up enough cash to outfit four Little League teams — the Yankees, the Cardinals, the Reds, and the Cubs. The uniforms were genuine (none of that cut-rate T-shirts and white socks trash) but since they were for miniature players, letter-space on the jerseys was at a premium and the Cardinals had to be Cards and the Yankees Yanks. Bruiser was a Yank and proud of it.

That would have dismayed Colonel Edens, one of his great-grampas and the obligatory family Confederate hero, but the South had changed so by Little Bruiser's time that he wasn't even aware of the old aversion to the Yankee name. His South wasn't the lotus ruin of Thomas Dixon Jr. or Octave Thanet. It had sloughed the role of sepulcher of the sacred rebellion, haunted by nigras and buzzed by the blue-tailed fly. The Civil War might as well have been the Trojan War for all Bruiser knew or cared, and Yankees were the New York baseball team and no longer a shibboleth for lynchbait. Ruth and Gehrig had redeemed the Yankee name so that even in Sheridan, Arkansas, in the early Nineteen Fifties it could be spoken respectfully without some carbuncled red calling for the tar-bucket and robing up in mammy's sheets.

To be a Yankee meant to Little Bruiser to be one of the immortals. It was a way to win the notice of the multitude, and the applause of the multitude if applause was deserved, without having to resort to buffoonery or derring-do, and without having to trust to pure luck. When he put on that precious uniform for the first time, Little Bruiser knew he wasn't a full-fledged Yankee yet, only a Yank; but he was on his way.

The Little League opening-day festivities in Sheridan were splendider than any county fair or car wreck that Bruiser had ever seen. They climaxed with a big pre-game parade from the Grant County courthouse to the ball field, a distance of about a mile. Five dozen Yanks, Cards, Reds and Cubs marched proudly in that parade. Proudly, but without much order or precision. Because the new uniforms were all-wool, and this being a hot day in June, the hike was characterized by a lot of scratching, squirming and fainting.

Bruiser avoided the indignity of a faint or puke, but he had other difficulties. He was one of two Yank contenders for the position of catcher ("hindcatcher," they called it then), and his new gear included a plastic cup inside his athletic supporter for protection against foul tips. Nobody told him he could wait until just before the game to slip the cup into place, so he wore it through that long day of public activities and during that mile-long trek across Sheridan. By the time he arrived spraddle-legged at the ball park, his little groin was so chafed that he wouldn't be able to walk naturally for a month, much less run out a bunt. He tried to participate in the pre-game warmups, but his coach was a compassionate man and, to Bruiser's horror, required him to sit out that epochal opening game against the mighty Cards.

That game was still a scarlet wound on Bruiser's memory when he recalled it thirty years later.

There was a stand of tall sycamore trees out beyond right field, and their long shadows stole ever so slowly up the first-base line, finally shading home plate and then the bleachers behind the chickenwire screen from the pitiless summer sun. The evening star made its appearance before Bruiser got the call at last to take his turn at bat.

It was Sheridan Little League policy to permit every player to bat at least once in every game, even those who, as the saying went, couldn't hit a bull in the butt with a bass fiddle. This policy was supposed to promote good sportsmanship, the democratic spirit, the work ethic, and such. In reality, it was a nuisance to the good ball players, the coaches and the spectators — a sop for the scrubs to keep them deluded and to keep their mommas and daddies off the coach's back. The coach asked Bruiser if he wanted to give it a try, and Bruiser did and didn't.

For two hours, he had fidgeted there at the end of the bench, chewing on sprigs of grass and entertaining Yankee visions. With every crack of somebody else's bat, he ached for the chance to go out and show that great throng who he really was, the future Dickey or Elston Howard or Mantle or Dimag, cocooned yet but Yankee through and through. But if he went to bat now, they would think he was just one of the scrubs. Also, the Cards were so far ahead on the scoreboard that he couldn't influence the game no matter what he did, and even if he hit a screamer he wouldn't be able to show his Yankee stuff on the basepaths because of the angry raw meat between his legs. So he equivocated: should he bat? should he put the Yankee in him to such a premature, unfair test?

He skipped the showing-off ritual in the on-deck circle and advanced directly to the batter's box in a ginger waddle. His pained and awkward gait drew some chortles from the grandstand and inspired no terror in the opposing pitcher, a lanky southpaw fastballer named Wallace Freeman. Bruiser tasted copper and bile and the top of his head threatened to blow his wraparound batting helmet off: this was the first moment of high drama in his young life. All the Yankee lore, all the Yankee instinct, all the Yankee dedication had to be concentrated now and brought to bear on the moment in thoughtless and exquisite execution. Dig in, then relax and let the Yankee show his stuff.

He tried to ignore the advice and criticism aimed at him from the bench and the bleachers — from the analysts and commentators sitting and squatting and leaning along the foul-line fences. He tried to block out all the non-essentials — the whoopers and know-it-alls, the coaches and players, the outfield fences which suddenly seemed five miles away, the sting in his groin, the prospect of ignominy if he struck out. He tried to block out all of the world and the evening except for that narrow tube of space between the Louisville Slugger/*Billy Martin* label of his twenty-nine-inch bat and the cobra crook of Wallace Freeman's throwing arm. He would be matador to the Wallace Freeman bull; he would be St. George and that left arm, with its wicked snap, throwing smoke, would be his dragon. Concentration, Bruiser. Come babe, come boy.

God love him, he *tried* to concentrate. He did his damndest to squeeze his attention and his reflexes into that tunnel where boys become Yankees. But the sizz and whap of the Freeman fastball dumbfounded him, and the shouts of the leaners and squatters, like crank telegrams to the doomsday war room, kept getting through.

"Don't hitch your swing!"

"Eye on the ball now!"

"You won't hit diddly-doo till you choke up on that bat."

He worked the count to two balls, two strikes, by simply standing in the box agape, like a pint-size replica of a Cooperstown statue. Only on the fifth pitch did he begin to feel the grip of fright and eagerness loosening; he got a slight sense of the rhythm, the flow, the ouevre, the metabolism of the game-situation, the *life*-situation; and that excited him so much that he barely checked his swing on ball three, which hit the dirt a foot in front of the plate. But check it he did, and hope began to flower in the Bruiser breast. Wallace Freeman wasn't so tough. With the count full now at three-two, Ol' Lefty wouldn't be able to nibble at the corners or play it cute with another go-fer pitch; he'd have to bring one of those blue-darters right into the Bruiser wheelhouse, and Bruiser might just lose it for him. Come on, Lefty, let's have your best shot, about peter high and right down the pipe, and it'll still be rising when it clears that sycamore beyond the Western Auto sign in right center.

Little Bruiser wasn't just mooncalfing here, like the Great Oz. He meant Yankee business. He could hardly wait for that payoff pitch.

But the worm of doubt is all-corrupting, and if Little Bruiser was bearing-down serious about sending a screamer out over that sycamore, he was also praying like a son-of-a-bitch for a walk. A walk would be redemption, or at least absolution. It wouldn't win him any glory but it wouldn't confirm that crowd's notion that he was just one of the scrubs. The future Yog or Mick or Moose would still be in the cocoon, but he wouldn't be *dead* in the cocoon. Wasn't it an axiom in the lore that a walk was as good as a hit?

Alas, the payoff pitch was a prodigy, even for Wallace Freeman. It was a howitzer shot, Durenesque, Koufaxian. Bruiser didn't even see it, although he would see it a thousand times in the decades to come, looming like an asteroid in the slow-motion freeze-frame replay that endured unerasable in his mind. It was right down the middle, all right. . .a good eighteen inches over Bruiser's head.

All his discipline, all his discretion, all his sandlot savvy were for naught.

He whiffed at it.

He whiffed at it with no more effort than a cattail waving at a passing train.

There was an instant when the Yankee dream petitioned God in Heaven for a reprieve. Maybe a foul tip. Maybe the ball got past the catcher. Maybe he had checked his swing in time.

Alas, no.

Little Bruiser had fanned.

He had fanned preposterously on a stepladder pitch.

Suckered by a tomwalker fastball! O *shame!*

There were no recriminations from the bleachers or the bench. No jeers or told-you-sos. The game was already lost anyway. A few of the leaners and squatters traded smug glances but that was all: yep, the hitch; the not choking up on the bat; whatever. Just a routine K by a routine scrub.

Wallace Freeman spat confidently, giving himself the credit.

Bruiser hustled back to the bench. It was required to hustle even when you fanned. Even when your crotch was on fire. Always gotta hustle, men! So he hustled. But it didn't feel like the noblesse oblige hustle of a Yankee or even a Yank. It felt like the clumsy scurrying hustle of a scrub.

Immediately after the last out of the last inning, Bruiser scrub-hustled out to the family auto and climbed in the back seat and wept forlornly. He didn't know why. Because he had betrayed his Yankee self. Because he imagined his Yankee self might be lost to him now forever. Woe!

Ah, but at ten, a Yankee vision is regenerative, like a chameleon's tail.

He was through bawling by the time the other family members got to the car, and during the ride home, listening in the dark to the big-league game on the car radio, Bruiser patched his broken confidence back together again, and imagined it as good as new.

CHAPTER THREE

Love and Morbidity

Once during his adolescence, Bruiser tried to find in the dictionary all the words that might suggest the vastness of his misery. *Titanic* and *gargantuan* were not adequate: he was much more miserable than either of them. He was more than humongously miserable. More than stupendously. Intergalactically wasn't the half of it. Here's Job on his ashdump with boils and the runs commenting on Adolescent Bruiser: "Boy, and I thought *I* had it bad!"

Biochemistry must have caused this change. It was surely glandular, although Bruiser was given later on to describing it in Marxian terms (about halfway between Karl and Groucho) as something of a personalized class struggle. "I was a plump little peasant who aspired to the bourgeoisie," he would say. "That's the whole dumb story of my youth, and probably the decisive influence on the rest of my life, too, I'm embarrassed to say."

Whatever the cause, Bruiser had developed by his fourteenth birthday a titantic or gargantuan inferiority complex. He became convinced that his classmates and contemporaries thought of him as a clod or a homo or a big dope. He thought they laughed at him behind his back. He thought they laughed about the way he looked and dressed and walked and talked and drank Cokes and got B+'s on most of his tests. He thought they laughed at him because his family was poor. He thought they *really* laughed when they saw him with a new haircut.

These were earnest beliefs, and even if the snubs were mostly imagined, that didn't make them hurt any less. One indication of the genuineness of his anguish was that Bruiser developed a speech defect — a slow and painful way of talking, afflicted at times by a serious stammer — that he never did completely conquer. Only around his family and Travis, and later Scamp, could he talk at all comfortably, without that burning self-consciousness that made so oppressive the life that once had seemed so fine.

Travis was better known as the Great Travis Shellnut. That was what he called himself. He was Adolescent Bruiser's counselor in the mysterious and elusive ways of popularity. He was the same age as Bruiser, and lived just up the road from the home place. He had as much reason as Bruiser to be demoralized by the peer pressures and warped expectations of adolescence, but he wasn't. Travis was irrepressible. This is what he told the school guidance counselor about his career plans: "I guess I'll probley be the new Elvis. With a rhinestone suit and ten million girls thinking I hung the moon. Then I'll get me a ranch and fly around it in my plane all the time like Sky King. But first I'm dropping out of school after the eleventh grade and joining the U.S. Marines."

Travis was forever plotting famous sexual conquests and his plans always included a choice morsel for Bruiser. He was determined to rescue Bruiser from the shyness and gloom, and he refused to let Bruiser's chronic pessimism faze him.

"It's just hopeless," Bruiser would moan. "I've done everything you told me, but it's not any use. I've learnt how to smoke and how to wear my blue jeans so they don't ride up in my crack. I go around blowing into my hand to make sure I don't have rotten breath, and I rub my nose every five seconds all day to make sure no boogs are hanging. When I get a sickening looking pimple, I play sick and stay home from school, and if I have to go back before it gets well, I walk around all day holding my hand over the part of my face it's on, trying to act like it's natural to go around all day with my hand covering up part of my face. I make fun of homos and don't hang around with anybody like Wally Cleaver. When I'm around somebody I'm trying to impress, I try to talk about drag-racing and rock-and-roll and making out. I know all the words to the Top Twenty, and I hate I can't dance, but it's hard to learn dipping and pushing when my partner's a damn doorknob that keeps falling off in my hand."

Travis would listen to this and say, "In two or three weeks me and you'll be the greatest studs ever to come out of Sheridan High School. They find out what we got to offer, they'll be formin' long lines."

To be recognized as a stud was the surpassing ambition of all the fourteen- and fifteen-year-old boys that Bruiser knew. A stud was a boy cultivating the look and manner of a certain species of hoodlum, emanating an air of criminal potential and wearing on one shoulder at least one smooth-skinned girl from a family well-off enough to put on airs. The stud had a name for chuggalugging beers and for never avoiding a rumble. A toothpick girdered his half-smirk. His intelligence, if not in obvious remission, was never brought out for public display. No Sheridan stud, for example, had ever been known voluntarily to have quoted Tennyson. But he knew the extremest subtleties of clutch-boxes and manifolds, and in the gunslinger tradition that prized the horse above the wench, his only true devotion was to his wheels. The car he drove was his own and he had souped it up and chromed it up himself. By day, he was taciturn, even sullen, but he was Lord of the Sheridan Night, peeling rubber, revving up and then purring down, the staccato growl of his cut-out muffler and custom pipes echoing through the dead late-night streets like the roar of a beast on the prowl.

Even if they'd had the grunt and the ducktails and the other requisites of studdom, Bruiser and Travis still would have been damned because neither of them had a rod. Without a car, they couldn't cruise around town half the night, honking and waving at the others who were scoring popularity points by cruising around, honking and waving. They couldn't tool out to the drive-in cafe on the Fordyce highway and park there and sit out on the hood half the night looking bored in a up-and-coming-stud way. And the real tragedy of carlessness: they couldn't ask girls out on dates.

At fourteen, fifteen, sixteen, Bruiser didn't have access to a car because the family no longer even *had* a car. Sister Nita and Brother James had grown up and moved away and taken with them the cars that they had worked as teenagers to buy, and that left only Daddy Joe's ancient battered pickup, which looked like it ought to have about nineteen Mexican illegals hanging on to its runningboards and tailgate. And Bruiser couldn't even get access to *that!* Damn old Daddy Joe had the quaint opinion that an automobile was a contraption for taking people somewhere they had good reason to want to go. He said it wasn't a play-pretty for young'uns to piddle around in, whizzing here and there like bats, burning up gasoline for no discernible purpose except to take money from a low-paid Arkansas sawmill worker and give it to John D. Rockefeller's boys to cram into their giant money sacks up in New York City, New York.

"I tried to reason with him, Travis," Bruiser whined, "but he just laughed and told me I needed a car like he needed another rupture. You know what he said? *Eighteen!* Said I could start driving at *eighteen!* He might as well have *shot* me. I don't even plan on *living* that long."

"Yeah, it's hell all right," Travis said. "But you might as well not sweat it. I'll think of something."

While Bruiser sank ever deeper into adolescent despondency, Travis learned to play a variety of musical instruments, including the harmonica and the uke, and to perform such U.S. Marine feats as doing a hundred one-handed push-ups in a row with each hand; and meantime he continued indefatigably planning non-car seductions, orgies and gangbangs, and instructing Brusier in the essential lore of larval Sheridan society — the two of them sitting in their treehouse with their feet hanging off, smoking cigs that Travis had stolen from his deadbeat Uncle Amos.

"I've heard about French kissing," Bruiser told him once. "You know what that is?"

"Shoot, yeah," Travis said. "I know ever'thing."

"What is it, then?"

"It's where you stick your tongue in a girl's mouth."

"Aw, you're lying. Nobody'd do that."

"A Frenchman would. You would too if you could find some big old fat girl that'd let you."

"I wouldn't neither. I'd do a lot of things but not that."

"Yeah you would. Cause it's the first step in getting 'em hot. They can't put.out if you don't get 'em hot."

"I'd get hot too if somebody jammed their tongue in *my* mouth."

"Naw, this is a different kind of hot. It's like warming up your arm before you pitch. If you try to do it before they're hot, it's raping, and you can get sent to the electric chair for that."

"You mean they could *kill* me for not jammin' my tongue in a girl's mouth?"

"They could, but you'd probably get off. Mostly all they kill for rapin' is nigs."

There was no important question Travis couldn't answer, no vital mystery he couldn't solve, whether it concerned menstruation, circumcision, spark-plug deposits, Buddy Holly or how to keep your Vitalis from attracting bees. But then one day Bruiser precipitated a crisis that defied even Travis.

"I knew you was morbid," Travis said, "but this beats it all. I don't know if *Zorro* could rescue you from this."

What Bruiser had done, he had fallen in love.

He had fallen in love with one of those smooth-skinned girls who are born popular. She had a family well-off enough to put on airs, and already, at fourteen, she tooled around in her own car, honking and waving. She was all of Bruiser's aches and longings suddenly manifest; his best imaginings transformed by some wonderful and punishing magic into actual flesh and personality. It made him dizzy just to know she existed in the same world he inhabited, and it also made him want to vomit and flog himself with Lash LaRue's bullwhip and crawl off somewhere and just *die* — because he had learned that she was herself already in love. With somebody else.

She was in love with a senior-class stud named Sonny Gruber, who had the dream job of clerking at the auto supply store. Sonny was retarded-looking, in Bruiser's opinion, but he had a four-barrel '55 Chevy with no hood and a twin exhaust and a pair of giant foam-rubber dice hanging from the rear-view, and Bruiser knew he would never be able to compete against that.

"I still can't see why she'd pick somebody like him," he told Travis.

"What I hear," Travis said, "it's probley that big wart on the end of his ten-inch pecker."

"You're just makin' that up."

"That's what I heard. Heard they call 'im Smokehouse in gym class. You know why? Cause he's got so much meat hangin'."

"You're lyin' and you know it."

"Well, he does have a rod that'll lay down ten yards of rubber in a second and he smokes Camels without queer-lippin' em."

"So what?"

"That's what they want. They think it beats somebody that goes around actin' like a goddam mummy."

"I don't go around actin' like no mummy."

"Yeah you do. You act like the mummy of a goddam ba*boon*."

"You can just kiss my ass, then. I'm sorry I even told you about it."

"Aw, I apologize. I just wish you wouldn't be so morbid. You know I'll think of some way out of this."

"Naw, just forget it."

"You're the one needs to forget it. You don't need love. Love's something you work up to. Need to do a lot of samplin' first. Make sure you find something that fits and don't smell like a damn old sardine can, that's what Uncle Amos told me. Fallin' in love now means you'll miss out on all the hogs you might have half a chance with."

"I didn't fall in love with 'er on *purpose*."

"All right, here's what we got to do. You go up to 'er after algebra tomorrow and say, 'Hey, Goodlookin', let me carry them books for you. You want a stick of Doublemint?' "

"I couldn't do that."

"Why not?"

"I just couldn't."

"All right, let me handle it then. Maybe I'll start a rumor that *you*'re the one with the wart. Maybe that'd do the trick."

But simply starting a wart rumor wasn't dramatic enough for Travis. He did something considerably more horrible than that.

"You did *what*?" Bruiser said, feeling the crush of a titanic, gargantuan humiliation.

"I just went up and told her," Travis said. "I said, 'Hey, I know this mummy in the tenth grade that'd pay a dollar a quart to drink your bathwater.' "

"Oh, God!"

"What's wrong with that?"

"God, I'm going over to Buie Funeral Home right now and climb in a casket and close the lid."

"Don't you even want to know what she said?"

"Please, Travis, don't tell me what she said. I mean it, I'll upchuck all over the place."

"All she said was, 'Hmmm, he's kinda cute.' "

"She didn't say that."

"Yeah she did."

"No she didn't. You didn't even talk to 'er."

"She said you reminded 'er a little bit of Tony Curtis. Who's that?"

"Tony Curtis?"

"That's what she said. She's a pretty good old girl. I didn't even have to tell 'er about your wart."

"I don't have no wart."

"*She* don't know that."

"I don't want 'er lovin' me cause of some damn wart."

"I told you, I didn't even have to *tell* 'er about the wart."

"It's embarrassin' enough without that."

"All I said was, 'He may be a mummy, but you never seen such a pole on a white boy in your life.'"

"You're lyin'. You didn't even talk to 'er."

"Okay, I didn't talk to 'er."

"Did you talk to 'er really, no lie?"

"Yeah, I kicked the door down for you. Now it's up to you."

"What am I supposed to do? I'd ask 'er to go ridin' around with me sometime but I don't feel like five years in reform school for stealin' a car."

"*She's* got a car, fool."

"Yeah, I can see it now — askin' 'er out on a date and then sayin', 'Oh, by the way, what time are you pickin' me up?'"

"You know what you need? You need somebody to just stomp your pitiful butt. I'm never rescuin' you from nothin' again, not even if you beg."

"Just tell me one thing."

"I ain't tellin' you nothin'. Or if I do, I'm chargin' you five dollars. Nobody appreciates first-class rescuin' when it's free."

"Just tell me if you really talked to 'er."

"Yeah, I talked to 'er. Now where's my dough."

"Dough?"

"Five bucks."

"I ain't payin' five bucks for a lie."

"All right then, I *didn't* talk to 'er. That's *ten* bucks."

"I knew you didn't talk to 'er."

"That's right. And you owe me fifteen."

"Tell me the exact words of what she said."

"You can't afford twenty bucks. How much cash you got on you right now?"

"Countin' all my gold and silver and diamonds and yachts and mink coats — twenty three cents. But I got two Tootsie Roll Pops."

"What flavors?"

"One orange and one grape."

"I'll give it to you word-for-word for the grape."

"I already licked off of the grape."

"You did not. You just want to stick me with a damn old orange."

"All right. But you better not lie."

Bruiser reluctantly handed over the grape.

"Okay, here's the deal," Travis said. "When she drives up at school tomorrow, you go over and say, 'Hey, honey, I'm the one you've heard about with the giant pole and the wart.'"

Travis already had the grape sucker in his mouth, so what could Bruiser do?

That's the authentic story of how it came about that Bruiser met the love of his life. He knew there was only one way to find out for sure, so he sought her out between classes the next day, and, blushing like a sunset and willing his stammer down, he forced his mouth to say: "Listen, uh, I don't know what Travis told you and all, but, uh — "

Before he could choke up and disgrace himself forever, she interrupted to say: "Has anybody ever told you you remind 'em a little bit of Tony Curtis?"

At that moment, another Bruiser appeared. The morbid old caterpillar broke its cocoon and made its metamorphosis: love had given it wings.

CHAPTER FOUR

Ear Crunches

Bruiser knew from the start that she was the love of his life. He showed her picture to his mother and said, "This is the girl I'm going to marry someday." His mother showed the picture to his father, and Daddy Joe handed it back to Bruiser with this observation and query: "She's a pretty little scamp, all right. What does she see in you?"

That question would haunt Bruiser for years. What *did* Scamp see in him? It couldn't have been his rugged good looks, which were closer to Tony the Tiger than Tony Curtis, and it seemed unlikely that she would have been attracted by his lack of charm, lack of muscularity, lack of a car, or lack of a giant pole lacking a wart. Bruiser assumed it was simple pity, and he dreaded the day when some Paris would come along and steal her away.

He was surprised when a week passed and she hadn't thrown him over for a stud. A month passed, and they were still together. And then it was a year. Then a decade, and a *second* decade, and he was willing finally to acknowledge that her attachment to him might be serious. It took that long for him to get up the nerve to ask her what it was that she had seen in him in the first place.

"I thought you'd make pretty children," she said.

It was a typically sensible answer. The biological wisdom of it revealed an instinctive feminine shrewdness that cut right through the balladeer mawkishness about trew, trew luv. But Bruiser didn't know whether he should feel flattered or insulted.

"Is that *all*?" he said. "I mean, I appreciate it, but a man likes to think he has a little bit of animal magnetism or something like that."

Scamp shrugged, and Bruiser affected a minor pout.

"Well, there *was* one other thing," she said, trying to be conciliatory.

"What?"

"You do have nice little ear crunches."

"Ear crunches?"

"Yeah, they're real cute."

Bruiser inspected his ears in the mirror. He could find no protuberances or juttings or nodes that might be considered "crunches."

"I don't see a thing," he said.

"They're right there," Scamp said, pointing vaguely.

Bruiser never was able to spot them, and eventually he gave up trying. Love is a mystery and he didn't want to press his luck. But it remained a source of wonder to him that so much of a man's fate could hinge on something that completely escaped the attention of Plato, Avicenna, Li Po, Shakespeare, Kierkegaard, Dostoevski, Freud, and Pogo:

Ear crunches.

CHAPTER FIVE

Football When It Is Bad

It is halftime in the locker room of the Sheridan High School Yellowjackets football team during Bruiser's senior year. The Yellowjackets are losing another game — something like their twentieth in a row. The players, including Bruiser, No. 80, offensive end and defensive outside linebacker, are sitting slumped on the scattered benches with their heads hung. Coach walks among them, pacing, preoccupied, his eyes narrowed to a squint but agleam from a private inferno. He says nothing for a time and the locker room is hushed. Then he murmurs a single word.

"Pain," he murmurs.

He paces more before he   says it again, louder this time, angrily.

"Pain!"

"Where is it, Crutchfield? Where is it, Thornton? Aker? Burns? Anybody...where is it? That football field out there is life — did you know that, Shofner? It's life. And do you know what life is? It's pain. Pain! I've tried to prepare you girls for it. Tried to teach you that glory comes only to him who can grin down pain with bloody gums. Where's the bloody gums? I'm not seeing bloody gums out there. All I'm seeing is unbusted lips. Quiver lips, just like you see on one of these streetcorner fruits. Are you a fruit, Plumley? Are all of you fruits? Pain, fruits! Football is life and life is pain! Inflict it! Embrace it and give it back with interest. Pain! That's what I want to see in this second half — pain! Are we clear on that? — pain! Pain!

Now before we get those helmets back on, let us pray."
Coach always concluded these spiels with a team prayer.
"Lord, we ask thy blessing on this team in this upcoming second half. With thy divine help and guidance, I'll turn these whiney little cocksuckers into football players yet. In Christ's name, amen."

CHAPTER SIX

At Frog Level

At age eighteen, Bruiser went off to college to become a chemist.

Not that he had developed an interest in the elemental composition of things. Nor had he been lured to science by all the post-Sputnik promotion of science education. Nothing as sensible as that. What it was, was this:

His mother had got him a chemistry set for Christmas when he was twelve years old, and he had promptly mixed some of the chemical powders into a vile goo. This goo smelled so bad that his mother made him take it out of the house and dump it in the yard. It killed some grass and zinnas, and made Moe the cat sick. Apparently that was such an interesting experience that Bruiser decided to make chemistry his life's work.

So many of the big decisions that make us what we are at forty, at fifty, at sixty-two, and at eighty-eight, looking back and wondering where the hair, the teeth and the time went, are made just this ignorantly, this unsuspectingly, by eighteen-year-olds. The child *does* father the man, an amazing and ludicrous way to run a life. It wouldn't cost God anything to let us reverse the procedure, so that the old geezer, or at least the *grown* one, could lobby or even coerce the boy whose whimsy had defined his life and most likely cursed it. If Reason were enthroned, that's how it would be. But as it is, we learn the useful stuff too late, and all we can do with it then is share it with those for whom it's *not* too late, and of course they don't want to hear it, and even if they did, what would we say to them: "*Chem*istry, Bruiser? For god's sake, *why*?" He dropped chemistry after his first semester at college and resolved to become a member of some other profession. Chemistry's successor was theology. Then wildlife biology. Then astronomy, geology, running a bulldozer, hustling pool, and others, none lasting much more than a week. The college he attended wasn't a distinguished one. Most of its teachers were failed something elses, and its administrators had a dromedary look and air about them. The college had a mule for a mascot. Its athletic teams were called the Muleriders. Its student newspaper was called *The Bray*. These are facts. Wouldn't old Bruiser have blushed if they had been revealed later on during his hoity-toity sojourn in high society! But at the time they were only a minor embarrassment. Bruiser had, after all, just got off the flatbed at Collegeville, and he made one of life's commonest and most unwarranted assumptions — that the people in charge had some intelligence and taste, and good reasons for doing things the way things were done.

The college was in the small south Arkansas town of Magnolia. The countryside around Magnolia was extremely flat, so the early settlers named their original village Frog Level. Frog Level, Arkansas. Not far from Hurrah City, Rough and Ready, and Ultima Thule. All of those were Arkansas towns but conventional people renamed them and the college got a conventional name, too. But here's what Bruiser always put on his resumes:

Attended Frog Level A&M, not far from Ultima Thule, Arkansas.
Bruiser's higher education included these courses:
Business 101.
Sociology 101.
Speech.
Modern Dance.
He didn't learn how to make money in the business class, and sociology was all charts and graphs, one of which informed him that there were ten "life-cycle stages," each with its own "major dilemmas of goal differentiation and integration." He was near the end of the "late adolescence" life-cycle stage, he learned, and his major dilemmas of goal differentiation and integration were "autonomy and intimacy." When he moved on to the "young adulthood" stage directly, his major dilemmas of goal differentiation and integration would be "self-determination, belonging or

connectedness."

Bruiser had no way of knowing that these big old smooth-sounding words were as empty as big old cardboard boxes, so he took comfort in their indication that there were experts who could examine his life at any point and tell him who he was and what he ought to be doing with himself. He resolved to work on his intimacy and autonomy, but wasn't quite sure how.

Still self-conscious about his afflicted voice, Bruiser refused to make any speeches in the speech class. When his turn came, he handed out mimeographed copies and then sat down. His classmates, after reading such a speech silently at their desks, sometimes gave him an ovation. He was never sure whether or not this was a derisive gesture.

He did fine in Modern Dance after he learned to pretend that the girls he was required to dance with were loose doorknobs. That didn't take much pretending with some of them.

Another course was Journalism 101, with Professor J. Stanley Hipp, a dapper little old man who wore a monocle and looked like Damon Runyon and claimed to be the only person who had ever understood what James Joyce was getting at in *Finnegan's Wake*, including James Joyce. Professor Hipp said he wouldn't disclose the secret even if someone pressed him, which, insofar as anyone knew, no one ever had. Professor Hipp didn't appreciate the way modern journalism was going. "Don't give me any of that cut-and-dried Hemingway drek in this class!" he proclaimed. "Give me Proust!"

Bruiser's favorite Frog Level course was a History of Western Civilization taught by a hard-looking woman with fright-wig red hair. Her name was Instructor Harlow. It was her theory that the key to understanding the rise and decline of the West was to know who got laid by whom, when, how often, and how satisfyingly. Harlow called this a Freudian view of history. She devoted much of her lecture time to telling the class how she went to Acapulco every summer to conduct intense personal research into the Freudian view of history.

Her chaperone for the Acapulco trips was Instructor Hornaday, who taught Bruiser's freshman English class. It was Hornaday's theory that the key to understanding the development of both English and American literature, and perhaps Russian and certainly French, was to know who got laid by whom, when, how often, and so on. She called this a Hornaday view of literature. Bruiser was amazed that people as old as Instructors Harlow and Hornaday were still apparently actively interested in sex. Both of them had to be in the "full-maturity" life-cycle stage already, when the major dilemmas of goal differentiation and integration are "dignity and control." Neither of them could have been much under forty.

Bruiser stâyed a year at Frog Level, soaked up as much higher education as he thought he could stand, then quit the college life, thinking that he could establish his intimacy and autonomy and start making some progress on his self-determination, belonging and connectedness if he married Scamp and settled down and got a job. He was satisfied, by and large, with his Frog Level introduction to higher education, brief and eclectic as it was. He enjoyed coming home to Sheridan on weekends and being appalled that nobody in his family had ever heard of Albert Camus. He explained to them the importance of Camus's books, which he fully intended to read soon. He also shook his head in shame and pity that they didn't know the first thing about Proust, either. Here's what Daddy Joe had to say about Proust: "Maybe *he* could tell me what to do about this rupture of mine."

CHAPTER SEVEN

The Boy Who Launched Armageddon

Bruiser and Scamp were married in secret soon after Scamp's high school graduation, exchanging their vows before a justice of the peace in a country store somewhere in the Ozark Mountains. It was a romantic little ceremony. The altar was a pot-bellied stove. The justice of the peace was also the storekeeper, and he had to take time out from selling fish bait to read the nuptials. His wife served as a witness. "Take off your apron, Momma, and come on over here," he told her. "You can dust off them canned goods later."

Afterward, Scamp returned to the temporary custody of her unsuspecting parents while Bruiser went out looking for a job and a honeymoon home. His prospects weren't good. About all he had going for him was his car. It was a wheezing twelve-year-old Plymouth with ninety-four thousand miles on it. It was the color of fog and Bruiser called it the Phantom Rickshaw. He had rustled up enough loose change from odd jobs around Sheridan to salvage it from a scrap-metal dealer, and his mother, at great sacrifice, had slipped him a few dollars along to help him pay off the note. He muscled it around the nondescript towns and cities of middle Arkansas during the late summer preceding the Assassination, looking for steady work.

This was a good time to be out and about in small-town America. The shine of Camelot reached even the out-of-the-way places, and there was a bright expectancy in the air. Black people and women and students and consumers and environmentalists were just beginning to stir, preparing to assert themselves, and Bruiser was ready to assert himself, too, even if he wasn't sure what there might be in him that was assertable, much less assert-worthy. He felt the new world a-coming, and he was a young man on the move, ready to take his place in the new order.

The only employer who showed any enthusiasm, though, was a Navy recruiter desperate to meet a quota. He wanted Bruiser to sign up as a navigator/bombadier trainee in the Naval Air Corps. That sounded fine to Bruiser, who had nothing against seeing the world. The recruiter said sure, the Navy accepted married men, even preferred them. Scamp could live right on the base. They would be far away from the coming wrath of Scamp's parents, Bruiser thought, and her old man might think twice before murdering a U.S. serviceman.

Bruiser might have made a brilliant career as a specialist in dropping bombs and liquid fire on human beings. He would have completed his training just in time for the big push in Vietnam. And he probably would have liked the work. The optical and electronic gadgetry in the bombers, the mathematical challenge, the maps and charts, the unfolding orange flowers and white puffballs way down below, the high adventure in a faraway place, the sense of involvement in the group pursuit of a noble cause — he would have eaten that up. This was the same Bruiser who would soon take up the principle of reverence for life, and he liked to think in retrospect that he would have balked when the time came to jack that first bombs-away lever. But he wouldn't have balked. He might have balked at killing and hurting people in the more civilized old-fashioned manner of club and blade, but he could have done napalm without a qualm or squeam, and if it had come to that, he wouldn't have shied from serving as buttonman for a nuke. All of this would have progressed naturally and easily, and Bruiser, with not a mean bone in him, would have become history's last great butcher, the boy who launched Armageddon.

The recruiter arranged for him to take his pre-induction physical examination at Memphis, riding over from Little Rock in the drafty hold of a derelict Navy cargo plane. He was the only passenger in that part of the plane, and the ride was cold and lonesome. Hunkering there in the half-dark on a pile of old flight jackets, he felt like Jonah in the belly of the whale. The big empty plane, the Navy, the grown-up world — they seemed a succession of ever bigger maws yawning to swallow him up. He felt small and insignificant. His first real inkling of the enormity of human existence stole over him like the momentary chill of a ghost's passing. He sensed that he would never be able to live up to all the expectations or even the demands. There would be no more Great Travis Shellnut rescues, or there would always be one less than enough. He would have liked to have been able to cry.

He wouldn't have admitted it, but he was relieved when the Navy turned him down. The Memphis chest-thumpers discovered that one of his knees was all macaronied inside, an ironic disqualifying legacy from his late life-is-pain football coach, who surely would have been one of the great gung-ho gook-blasters of the domino war.

It was two months before he found work. He landed a job in Pine Bluff, one of the larger cities in Arkansas, only a half-hour's drive from Sheridan. He hired on as a rookie meter-reader for the Arkansas-Louisiana Gas Company. He did it reluctantly. He didn't aspire to be a gas-company meter reader, and he didn't want to live in Pine Bluff, whose first settlers didn't name it the Slough of Despond only because they were French and didn't think of it. He was so demoralized going to work the first morning that he just couldn't do it; he couldn't wheel into his assigned parking space and report for duty. Instead, he let the Phantom Rickshaw detour him through the outskirts of Pine Bluff and deliver him to the foot of the big bridge spanning the Arkansas River. He didn't realize until he saw the bridge that he intended to jump off of it.

Bruiser had never considered suicide before, and he didn't know what inspired him to consider it now, unless it was the Phantom Rickshaw's radio just having played "Running Bear" for him. "Running Bear" was a rock-and-roll classic. It told the story of two American Indian lovers, Running Bear and Little White Dove, who drowned themselves in a raging river. They didn't drown themselves for nothing. They proved an important point by going under and turning blue and bloating up and getting eaten by slimy turtles and horrible old gars. They shamed the world for being such a stupidly callous place. They taught it to better appreciate the poignancy of the plight of sensitive young people. Their gesture was moving and memorable because it was deliberate, unlike that of Romeo and Juliet, who just screwed up.

Bruiser pondered the leap for a long time. Two or three minutes at least. But he couldn't jump. For one thing, the Arkansas River wasn't the picturesque torrent of "Running Bear"; at that time, it was a damn old sewer, bearing detrius from as far away as Colorado, and it killed the Byronic fascination to think that he would probably start festering even before he drowned. Another deterrent was that he couldn't think up a sufficiently heartrending note.

In the end, he didn't even get out of the car. He just turned it around and chugged on into Pine Bluff. But he didn't stop at the gas-company office. He drove around for a time, irresolute and unthinking, looking at all the Negro hovels and muffler shops; then he parked the Rickshaw on Main Street and set out walking, with no destination in mind.

Next thing he knew, he was wandering through some cubicles in an old building that might have been a Victorian funeral parlor or an abandoned cotton gin. It turned out that these cubicles were the editorial offices of a daily newspaper, the *Pine Bluff Commercial*. A receptionist or secretary mistook him for a yam farmer who was due for an interview with Clarence Taylor, the newspaper's farm editor. She delivered him to Clarence's cubicle.

Clarence Taylor was a talkative, white-haired old man who reminded Bruiser of Walter Brennan, the movie actor. He told Bruiser to pull up a chair and take a load off his feet.

"Don't mind if I do," Bruiser said, having decided, with nowhere else to go, to play along with the masquerade. "I'm purt near wore out, traipsing around in these store boughten shoes."

Clarence got a kick out of that, and he and Bruiser exchanged some more back-forty pleasantries before Clarence got down to business.

"Well, did you bring it with you?" he said.

"I'm not sure," Bruiser said. "What's *it*, exactly?"

"The sweet potater!" Clarence said.

Bruiser didn't know anything about any sweet potato and soon had to fess up. Clarence was disappointed but didn't hold it against him.

"This old boy out at Rob Roy grew it," Clarence said. "They say if you hold a flashlight up agin' it, it casts a shadow that's a perfect silhouette of President Kennedy."

"I'd love to see that," Bruiser said.

"You said it!" Clarence said. "I thought maybe you'd bring it with you when you came in."

"'Fraid not," Bruiser said. "Sorry."

"Maybe next time."

"Maybe so."

While they talked about this horticultural miracle, a younger man was pacing back and forth just outside Clarence's cubicle. He reminded Bruiser of the White Rabbit in *Alice in Wonderland*: he seemed to have something urgent on his mind, and he appeared in a great hurry to go somewhere he couldn't remember.

"That's Gene Foreman, our managing editor," Clarence said. "He's well known throughout the world of journalism."

That was true. This was the same Gene Foreman who later became the distinguished managing editor of the *Philadelphia Inquirer*. He had come to the *Pine Bluff Commercial* by way of the *New York Times*, which had been shut down by a prolonged strike, marooning many notables like Gene at hinterland dailies and hebdomadals.

Clarence called this great celebrity into the cubicle.

"Gene, I want you to meet this young fellow," he said. "I thought he was our potater man but he's not."

"You wouldn't be the sportswriter by any chance, would you?" Foreman said to Bruiser.

"Which one is that?" Bruiser said.

"The one I've been praying would appear here out of thin air," he said. "Wow, it's football season already and I don't have sportswriter one."

"That's what all that pacing and muttering was about," Clarence explained.

"What are the qualifications?" Bruiser said.

"A measurable pulse," Foreman said. "Anything beyond that is negotiable."

Bruiser was almost numb with ecstacy.

"I was directed here by the shade of the late J. Stanley Hipp," he said. "When do I start?"

So it was that Bruiser stumbled upon an occupation, a career, as a hobo might unexpectedly come upon the stub of a first-rate stogie, as Sluggo in "Nancy" sometimes found in the debris of the city streets a windblown ten-dollar bill. Bruiser didn't deserve this prize, this bonanza, but he meant to make the most of it. He meant to become a sportspage phenomenon — Yankee, Proustian, unique.

CHAPTER EIGHT

Pressbox Greek

Not counting three-color comics and a few sluggish forays into required texts, Bruiser had got his high school diploma without ever having read a single book all the way through. Even *Peyton Place* lost him after the scene early on in which Rodney and Betty got into each other's drawers. Frog Level Bruiser's repeated assaults on Sartre's *Being and Nothingness* never got beyond the philosophical breastworks of page three, and a single paragraph by Henry James once vanquished a whole package of No-Doz.

Ed Freeman, one of the owners of the *Pine Bluff Commercial*, shamed Bruiser into learning to read. Ed knew the *Dialogues* of Plato better than Clarence Taylor knew parasites in hogs, and Ed's idea of job training for young journalists included heavy doses of Sophocles and The Iliad in addition to the who what where when and why. Ed thought his reporters and editors could learn something from the old Greeks about clear and logical thinking, and about the true dimensions and implications of seemingly routine news events.

Bruiser tried to read all the works that Ed recommended, and the long-term influence was remedial and constructive, but some of the short-term effects must have given Ed pause. Here is the lead, for instance, on one of the football game stories that Bruiser wrote for the *Commercial*:

Following the big loss to the Fordyce Redbugs Friday night, Coach Leon (Dub) Schwarzenagle walked out of the dressing room shaking his head, looking as dejected as Oedipus trudging off to Colonus.

Come to think of it, that lead gave Coach Dub pause, too. He phoned up Bruiser wanting to know who this guy Oedipus was that he was being compared to, and whether at this Colonus they had a "winning program."

NIGHT MOVES

Sick Bed
The Murder of Shorty Fudd
Nocturne in Z

CHAPTER NINE

Sick Bed

The honeymoon apartment wasn't exactly a dump, but a tyro sportswriter earning fifty-eight dollars a week couldn't expect swank. It was a three-room "efficiency unit" that had once been a one-car garage. It had a small parlor joined to a small bedroom by a smaller kitchen, and a built-on bathroom about the size of those in commercial airliners. As a child in Sheridan, Scamp had had a *playhouse* bigger than this apartment, but she never complained now of feeling cramped. She did name it Munchkin Manor, but intended no disparagement: it really did have the look of an erstwhile midget hive, and Bruiser found himself whistling "Whistle While You Work" a lot.

Bruiser's memories of the place twenty years later focused on the tiny bedroom, where he found not only nuptial bliss but also an appreciation for the wisdom of those old Greeks. They knew something about life, those old faggot winos did, that eluded the dour holy men of Judah. They knew it isn't so much an epic saga of tragic yearnings as it is a series of swift little kicks in the ass. They surmised that, in the boredom of immortality, the eternal gods invented practical jokes and then created people to have somebody to play them on. The bed itself led Bruiser to this understanding.

Something was wrong with the bed, and Bruiser couldn't figure out what it was. He assumed for a time that the trouble was mechanical — that there was a structural defect in the frame, or that the slats which held up the mattress and springs were too short. But he soon realized that here was no ordinary bed. It *looked* like an ordinary bed, but all the other evidence suggested a living being condemned to give the appearance of a bed — a poor damned soul sentenced on a whim to an eternity of holding people up off the floor while they snored, drooled on their pillows and emitted other substances, bruxed their teeth, and copulated. And the indignity or the absurdity or the tedium had to be just too much for it. It s problem was psychological, not mechanical. It had a screw loose, all right, but not a metal one.

It behaved just fine, this goddamned bed did, during the first few nights that Scamp and Bruiser occupied it. It kept its emotional distress to itself. But then one night at two thirty a.m. it threw out one of its slats. The clatter on the hardwood floor in the still of the small hours gave Mr. and Mrs. Bruiser a good fright, but they thought no more about it until the following night, when, again at two-thirty or thereabout, *several* of the slats fell out. That caused a brief scene in which Bruiser tried to convince both Scamp and himself that there was no logical way that the underbed commotion could have been caused by either large horrible rats or small clumsy burglars.

On subsequent nights, more and more of the bedslats got into the act, and they weren't content to cause only one disturbance per night. They did matinees and encores, full dress rehearsals and instant replays. Bruiser would drag in after a hard day and would retire with great foreboding, knowing that he would have to reassemble the entire bedworks at least three times before the rosy-fingered dawn. These night labors came to be quite a strain on him because he was working sixteen-hour days for his fifty-eight weekly dollar bills.

Of course the slats wouldn't fall out when he and Scamp first went to bed. No matter how athletic and rambunctious their pre-sleep activities, those slats beneath them were models of early evening discretion. You would have thought they would have supported an orgy. Circus tumblers, sex-crazed hippotami couldn't have shaken them loose. It was only after the lovebirds were well into the deep-sleep cycle of their repose that a slat would wriggle loose and clatter alarmingly to the floor. The noise would cause Scamp to jump, which would signal more slats to release their hold and follow their rowdy leader. Bruiser and Scamp would lie very still, hoping to hold the remaining slats in place by emulating rigor mortis. Bruiser tried to hold them in place by sheer strength of will, like Jackson at Chancellorsville; by a kind of prayerful telekenesis; by reminding them telepathically of the Dutch boy with his finger in the dike.

Sometimes, lying there warily, Scamp would whisper, careful not to move her lips: "I need to turn over."

"Scamp, if you love me, if there's a drop of the milk of human compassion in you, you won't turn over," Bruiser would whisper in reply.

After a while, she would whisper: "I've *got* to turn over."

"If you won't turn over," Bruiser would say, "I promise I'll talk to the landlord tomorow and *demand* a new bed."

"Shhhhh," she would say, almost inaudibly, meaning he should tone down his imploring lest vibrations of his voice spook the few remaining slats into the stampede.

But sooner or later, Bruiser would get a cramp in a toe, or Scamp would have to yawn, or one of them would drop back to sleep and turn over — and another slat would Geronimo.

And then another.

Bruiser would get up then and crawl under the bed. Trying to focus his eyes, trying to get alert enough to remember what he was doing, he would attempt to jimmy the prodigal slats back into place.

Then when he got back in bed, one would fall out again.

Sometimes it wouldn't wait until he was back in bed. It would fall out forthwith, hitting him in the eye or chipping one of his front teeth.

He couldn't reinsert the slats while Scamp was on the bed, so while he maneuvered down there on the floor, dodging falling slats, she would stand asleep nearby with her head against the wall. One time she forgot he was still under the bed; she crawled back into her place and a veritable forest of bedslats fell on Bruiser. A slat landslide or avalanche. Half asleep, Bruiser fought back.When he came to his senses, he was actually trying to *strangle* a slat. He got out from under the bed just before the mattress, the box springs, the covers, the pillows, and Scamp came tumbling through the bedframe to the floor.

"My God, I could have been killed under there!" he said. "I can see the headline now: KILLER BED OFFS SCRIBE."

Scamp had no comment on that because she had slept right through the crash.

But the landlord, whose bedroom abutted the apartment,

was awakened, and he came knocking at the Munchkin Manor door.

"Hey in there!" he shouted. "I know you two are new-lyweds but you got to keep it down. I'm a working man."

"We need a new bed," Bruiser yelled through the door to him.

"New bed? Hell, son, that bed's a heirloom."

"They don't make heirlooms out of pressed wood."

"Well you tear it up, I take the cost out of your deposit. Now keep it quiet over here."

Bruiser waited until the landlord was safely out of hearing, then said defiantly: "If you don't get us a new bed, one of these slats is going to be wearing your large intestine."

Scamp was still asleep when Bruiser got back to the bed-room. He got her up and told her about the tough stand he had taken against the landlord. Then he propped her up against the wall, reslatted the bed, and gingerly tested it out. The slats held, so he carefully put Scamp back to bed and lay down again himself.

He lay waiting.

The slats held.

"One of you bolshevik bastards go ahead and fall," he said silently.

But they held.

"Don't think I'll doze off and let you do it to me again."

But eventually he dozed off.

And when he did one of the slats fell.

Then another one.

There were times when, after reslatting the bed half a dozen times in a night, Bruiser resolved to fix the bed once and for all, and in the darkness before the dawn he could be seen beating on the heirloom with a hammer, tying it up with fishing line and coat hangers, indiscriminately nailing hinges and washers and fruit-jar lids on it while Scamp stood by, oblivious, sound asleep with her head against the wall. One night, in a delirious muddle, Bruiser tried, by the dawn's early light, to glue all the slats back in place with Elmer's Glue-All.

When Scamp roused to ask him what he thought he was doing, he said: "Never mind! Just tell me if the drugstore stays open this late."

"Drugstore?"

"Yeah, if this don't work, I want to try Poly-Grip."

The landlord refused to bring in a new bed, but one night during the customary beating and banging, he did bring in the police.

That got Bruiser riled, and he gave them a piece of his mind, such as it was, telling them that he paid their salaries and that they ought to be out catching child molesters instead of bothering law-abiding citizens who were merely trying to teach their delinquent bed a lesson.

In his mealy-mouth fashion, he waited until they were gone to tell them that, but at least he got it off his chest.

He wouldn't let Scamp call a bona fide repairman because it insulted his honor as a handyman that he couldn't fix something as simple as a mischievous bed. So they endured the bed's antics and tantrums, and Bruiser finally came to understand that tightening the frame or replacing the slats with longer ones wasn't the answer. The bed obviously had something on its mind, maybe an unresolved neurotic conflict peculiar to those condemned to be regarded as beds. It was a sick bed, on the verge of a breakdown.

Its problems were no fault of its own, Bruiser admitted that. Prankish deities were having sport with it. He wanted to be liberal-minded and let it work out its difficulties, but one night an allergy brought on a Bruiser sneezing fit and before morning he had chopped the bed to pieces with the landlord's woodpile axe.

CHAPTER TEN

The Murder of Shorty Fudd

The telephone in Munchkin Manor meant a lot to Bruiser and Scamp. It was their one link during Bruiser's long hours of wage-slavery. If fortune had robbed them of a honeymoon, they could at least ring up one another during Bruiser's coffee breaks and coo.

It was a plain old black dial telephone, mounted on the kitchen wall, and unlike the bed it seemed mechanically and emotionally sound. It had a good strong dial tone and a vigorous ring. It also had a number listed in the directory under somebody else's name, but Bruiser and Scamp didn't find out about that until after the installer was gone.

This was a day or two before Bruiser slew the bed. The time was again between the witching hour and dawn. He had already reslatted the bed twice and had just fallen into a wary doze when the telephone gave forth a robust ring. He thought at first that the *bed* was ringing — a new attention-getting, sleep-wrecking trick — but then the phone pronounced itself again, and Scamp got up and groped through the bedroom and into the kitchen to answer it.

"Hey, Sweetheart! How's tricks?" the cheery caller said.

Scamp was a veteran sleepwalker, and in the somnabulistic state she wasn't inquisitive or suspicious, so she replied with the dreamy candor of the not fully conscious: "Oh, fair. It's not Niagara Falls but we're getting by."

"Yeah, well, that's super, Doll," the caller said. "You know what Odysseus said — all us dogs will have our day. Let me talk to old Shorty for a sec, would ya?"

Scamp wandered back to the bedroom and nudged Bruiser awake. "It's for you," she told him.

Bruiser slouched to the telephone and mumbled a sleepy 'lo.

"Hey, Piss Trough! What's the good word?" the caller said.

"Piss Trough?" Bruiser said.

"Oh. What's the password this week?"

"Password?"

"Black is the color of my true love's hair? Or was that last week's? Double, double, toil and trouble? Why do we have to go through all this crap every time, Shorty? You know me. And all I want is fifty on Afterburner in the first at Liberty Bell."

"Who *is* this?"

"Who is *this*?"

"It's not Shorty, that's for sure. You got a wrong number."

"565-0909?"

"That's it, but there's no Shorty here."

"Oh, I get it. Somebody's there listening and you can't talk right now. It's not the cops, is it Shorty?"

"Yeah, it's the cops," Bruiser said, and he hung up the phone.

But it rang again before he could get back to bed.

When he answered it, the same caller said: "Listen, Shorty, if it's that two hunnerd I owe you, I'll get it to you first thing in the morning."

"This is not Shorty. Wrong number again."

"565-0909?"

"Bingo. And no Shorty."

"It's Shorty's number."

"I don't know what I can do about that."

"Shorty's real name is Elmer J. Fudd but he's embarrassed about it because of the cartoons, you know. I call him Shorty. Or sometimes Piss Trough. That's on account of he can stand on one side of the john and piss in the trough on the other. Fifteen, twenty feet away — he'll hit it dead center. Amazing. He don't like me calling him Piss Trough, though. Most of the guys call him Doc and he likes that. But mostly I just call him Shorty. Where is he?"

"I don't know the party you're trying to reach. Now quit bothering us."

"Jeez, what is it with you, Shorty? Is it them cops? If they're still there, I just called to give you this message: I've bought *fifty dollars* worth of plaster and I'm taking the *first* plane to Philly — one of them big jets with the *afterburners* — and I'm going to patch up the crack in the *Liberty Bell.* You get my drift?"

"I'll take care of it," Bruiser said, slamming the phone back onto the wall.

It rang again before he could finish a yawn.

"What is it now?" he answered gruffly.

"Sounds like you got a cold, Shorty. Them cops aren't torturing you or nothing, are they?"

"This is *not* Shorty."

"How come you're taking my bets if you're not Shorty?"

"I'm going back to bed now. And if you call this number again, I'll find out who you are and I'll hunt you down and rip your heart out and feed it to a stray dog. You got that?"

"Good old Shorty!"

"I'm serious, chump."

"If it's that two hunnerd, Shorty, it'll be there before the milkman."

"Would it help if I *begged* you to believe I'm not Shorty?"

"What is this, Shorty? I'd know that old molasses drawl anywhere. Remember the night we spent in the Bombay Bicycle Club in Toronto. Jeez, I'd never seen you *drunk* before. I mean, tipsy, sure. But *Jeez!* Tell you the truth, Shorty, I was a little scared."

"I've never been to Bombay."

"No, Toronto, Shorty. To*ron*to. King Edward Hotel, right? Them two crazy dames drove us all the way to Quebec City, and you jumped in the St. Lawrence below the Frontenac there, yelling you were going to swim all the way to France, retracing Cartier's route backward. Wow! Them was the days, eh Shorty?"

"I've got a tracer on this phone, you know."

"Cops are still there, right?"

"I never been to Bombay and I can't swim and I don't drink."

"Don't *drink*? Ho, ho, *ho!* Shorty the teetotaler!"

"I'm not Shorty."

"Come to think of it, you do sound hoarse for Shorty."

"I don't sound *anything* like Shorty, if you'll think about it."

"Ah, Shorty, you can fool some of the people some of the time, but this is *me*. Boot camp, remember? Iwo Jima. Singapore. We done *time* together. Unless them cops are still listening in. In that case, I'll go along, sure. Never seen the champion pisser before in my life."

"Listen to me. I just got this telephone installed and obviously the number used to belong to someone named Shorty or Elmer or Pisspot — "

"Trough."

"What?"

"Trough. Piss *Trough.*"

"Yeah, well, anyway, this isn't Shorty's number any more. I'm not Shorty and Shorty's not here. I don't *know* any Shorty. And I'm fast learning to *hate* Shorty, whoever he is. I'm putting him right up there with Hitler and baby-seal killers. I'm putting him right up there with *you*. I can't keep you from calling this number again, but if you do, I'm going to lie down on the floor and cry like a doorstep orphan. It'll break your heart to hear the kind of crying I'll do."

With that, Bruiser softly replaced the phone on the hook.

It rang again after, oh, two or three seconds. Bruiser decided to let it ring. He took very short naps between each ring. After the twelfth ring, he concluded that the caller wasn't going to give up. He lifted the receiver and replaced it. It rang again and he lifted and replaced it again. He answered it the next time.

"Are you trying to tell me this is not Shorty?"

"In the sincerest way I know how."

"You mean you're really not?"

"I do."

"You swear?"

"As God is my witness, I am not Shorty."

"Well put Shorty on then. I need to talk to him."

Bruiser sat back against the kitchen wall and heaved a great sigh. After a moment, the telephone receiver slipped from his hand and dangled down the wall like a small monk at the end of a bell rope. His chin dropped slowly to his sternum, his eyes fluttered, and he nodded off.

They didn't know all this right hemisphere/left hemisphere brain stuff in those days. Bruiser only knew that some of his best ideas drifted across his thinking during that woozy instant between waking and sleep. And one of those ideas lured him back from this snooze. Without opening his eyes, he felt for the dangling monk, found it and put it to his ear.

"Sorry," he mumbled into the mouthpiece, "Shorty can't come to the phone on account of he died."

"What!" the caller said.

"He died," Bruiser said, waking to the idea. "You know, Croak City. Tombstone Territory."

"Come on now, Fats, that's not funny."

"Fats?"

"That's another nickname Shorty goes by."

"Went by."

"What?"

"Went. Shorty is past tense now."

"Tell me you're just kidding."

"I'm not kidding. Shorty rolled snakeeyes this time. He pulled a deuce. Spread the word to his friends, would you?"

"Come off it now. Where's Shorty?"

"You know all those railroad crossings between Seventeenth Street and Sixth Street?"

"Yeah. So?"

"That's where he is."

"Where?"

"Smeared all along there. Shorty's not short any more. Mighty thin, but he's three-quarters of a mile long."

"Are you saying Shorty got hit by a *train*?"

"Sorry to have to break it to you."

"Jeez, I'm speechless."

"God, I hope so."

"Not Shorty! Not good old Piss Trough! You're putting me on."

"I don't even *know* you."

"Jeez, I'm a wreck. Shorty was a great man. I named my daughter after him."

"You named a little girl *Shorty*?"

"No, I named her Fudd. I wouldn't put a name like Shorty on a kid. Think of all the ridicule she'd have to take."

"Fudd is better than Piss Trough, I guess."

"Yeah, she's a great kid. Her mother's got her. They live in Racine, Wisconsin. But getting back to Shorty...Jeez, I'm a wreck. I don't mind telling you, I loved the man. I was afraid of something like this. Last time we talked, he was quoting Keats' *Ode to a Nightingale* and I thought to myself, uh-oh. That passage, 'Now more than ever seems it rich to die/To cease upon the midnight with no pain.'"

"I doubt he had much pain."

"He had enough while he was alive. He had gout, you know, like Dr. Johnson."

"We all have our crosses to bear. You want to hear about mine?"

"Sure, why not?"

"I'm working sixteen hours a day and I can't get any sleep at night because some gabby son-of-a-bitch keeps ringing my telephone."

"You know, Shorty had proof that Ben Jonson wrote seven of Shakespeare's plays. You'd call him up and first thing, right out of the blue, he'd say, 'Here's one I bet you didn't know: the planet Uranus used to be named Herschel.' You just don't come across a guy like that in this burg every Tuesday."

"He was something, all right. Now if you'll excuse me, I need to get back and finish the prayers I was saying for him. Good talking to you."

"Come on, Shorty, a joke's a joke, but this is *me* — "

Bruiser hit the disconnect button and quickly dialed the operator to ask if the telephone company could give him any relief. The operator was sympathetic but told him he would have to talk to someone in the business office, which opened at ten o'clock the following morning.

"Would it help if I told you I won the Congressional Medal of Honor?" Bruiser said.

But the operator had already buzzed off.

Bruiser knew nothing else to do but leave the phone off the hook for the rest of the night. He left the little monk dangling there on the bell rope and lumbered back to bed.

He soon discovered that the telephone company disapproved of its customers leaving their telephones off the hook. It disapproved so strongly that it caused a receiver left dangling to shriek after thirty seconds. The shriek was something like that of a police whistle or an elk. It wasn't as loud as an elk — or even a smoke alarm — but it was plenty loud in the dead of night in an apartment that was meant to be the housing for a medium-size cuckoo clock.

Eleven seconds after Bruiser got back in the bed, three seconds after he squirmed around and got situated, one second after he closed his weary eyes, one-eighth of a second after he caught the Lethan ferry — the telephone began to shriek.

He lumbered back to the kitchen and dialed the operator again. She told him that his options, until the business office opened at ten a.m., were five:

(1) He could allow the telephone to shriek and try to ignore it.

(2) He could wake up, get up, go into the kitchen, and depress the receiver hook every twenty-nine seconds all night.

(3) He could remove the telephone housing and try to muffle the bell clapper with cotton balls, chewing gum or ear wax.

(4) He could shoot the telephone at close range with a twelve-gauge shotgun.

(5) He could take his chances with the friends, relatives, clients and mourners of Elmer J. (Shorty) Fudd.

Bruiser depressed the hook and immediately the phone rang.

"Goddam it, Shorty's dead and I told you never to call this number again!" he shouted.

"Well!" the operator said huffily.

"Oh, I'm sorry. I thought — "

But she buzzed off again before he could apologize.

He depressed the hook and the phone rang again.

"I'm sorry, Operator," he answered. "I thought — "

"Listen, Doc, are you sure we're talking about the same Shorty?" the original caller said. "There's plenty of Shortys but I never heard of another real-life Elmer J. Fudd. That was his real name, you know. He was embarrassed about it because of the cartoons."

"So I heard," Bruiser said.

"Well, what about it?"

"I lied about him getting hit by a train."

"You did?"

"Yeah."

"Jeez, what a relief! I was calling to tell you, instead of the usual ashes-to-ashes, dust-to-dust crap, the minister ought to read this Matthew Arnold elegy called *Rugby Chapel.* It was one of old Piss Trough's favorites. He was sort of a somber guy. I'm not saying he didn't have a sense of humor. Not at all. Name a subject and he could tell you a joke about it. But underneath he was sort of melancholy. Like one of them old jazz musicians. There was something doomy about him, if you know what I mean. You want the truth, I think the man was a saint. But hey, why am I saying *was*? I guess he still is, eh? Put him on the phone, would ya? I need to talk to him."

"I lied about the train," Bruiser said. "The truth is, I murdered Shorty myself with my bare hands. And you know what else, vermin? You're next."

He dropped the receiver, letting the monk dangle, while he went to look for some cotton balls. He couldn't find any, so he wound up trying to muffle the bell clapper with some leftover raspberry Jell-o.

He finally cut the telephone wire with his pocket knife.

Before he got back in bed, he reset the alarm clock to give himself an extra half-hour, come the dawn, to reconnect, reinsulate and resolder the wire.

When he climbed back in bed, one of the slats fell out.

As soon as he got the wire reattached the next morning, the telephone rang. Bruiser picked up the receiver but before he could even say hello, a reedy, high-pitched voice said:

"You dirty killer, what have you done with my Uncle Elmer?"

"You're on the list, too, Wimp," Bruiser snarled. "Right after that poet bastard who didn't bring me the two hunnerd dollars he owes me."

"Why, you murdering animal!"

"Why, you little pissant!"

"Scum!"

"Pansy!"

"You won't get away with this!"

"Yeah, I will. And I'm coming over to your place right now to blow your wimp head off."

"You just try it!"

"I will, twit. Prepare to meet thy God."

Scamp, sitting at the kitchen table eating a bowl of corn flakes, listened to this madness with perfect aplomb. When Bruiser slammed the phone back on the hook, she said: "Who was that?"

"Oh, that was just Shorty's nephew."

"And you're planning to kill him?"

"Not really. I ought to, though."

"I don't guess I know him."

"He's a real pipsqueak. I bet the guys really kidded Shorty about him."

"I don't know Shorty, either."

"*No*body knew Shorty. He was a real mystery man."

"Was?"

"Got hit by a train. I told you about that last night. You kept saying, 'Too bad!' "

"I must have been dreaming about the wedding gifts we've got. Five toasters and not one coffee pot. You want some instant?"

"Shorty's real name was Elmer Fudd. He wasn't anything like the cartoon Elmer Fudd, but he couldn't show his face without somebody doing a Bugs Bunny what's-up-doc at him. Even bank tellers and hitchhikers and people like that. No wonder he was so doomy."

"Here, take my cup. I'll make me another one. You want some toast? I can make ten pieces at a time."

Bruiser sipped at the coffee and thought about Shorty. Some of it the midnight caller had told him, and some he must have just dreamed. He remembered that Shorty was supposed to be the true author of *Treasure of Sierra Madre* and of more than two hundred limericks attributed to Anonymous. Damon Runyon had made him famous for a time in *Blue Plate Special* as the Lemon Drop Kid. He was the one who had deflowered Jean Harlow on the bearskin rug, and he was married to Elizabeth Taylor but people had forgot about him when they lost count. There was some connection with Amelia Earhart and Judge Crater and Howard Hughes, and something about espionage in a pumpkin patch and an eighty-yard run against the Chicago Bears. It wasn't clear how he had wound up as a two-bit bookie in the Slough of Despond, but it had to do with drink, Arthur Rimbaud, and time up the river for a what's-up-doc that was one too many.

But it was time to go to work. It was Bruiser's task to relate not the deeds of the Shorty Fudds of this world but the deeds instead of varsity athletes who tried to cram at least five *you-knows* into every incomprehensible sentence they spoke.

It was several days before the telephone company got around to giving Mr. and Mrs. Bruiser a different telephone number. Bruiser got very little sleep during that time, but he found out many more interesting facts about the colorful life of Shorty Fudd, and he covered forty-nine bets, most of them on horse races but one by a black mortician who only wanted twenty-to-one — and Bruiser leapt on this — that somebody named Clay would beat Sonny Liston. This was an interesting man. He called up one day to say that he was taking an unscheduled vacation because he had just learned that it probably would be ten billion years, rather than seven as predicted earlier, before the sun entered the red-giant stage and incinerated the earth. In that same conversation, he told

Bruiser that the body of Queen Elizabeth I, who left instructions that she wasn't to be embalmed, swelled up and exploded so violently that it demolished the first coffin she occupied. This was a fact that Bruiser didn't know and might never have learned had he not murdered and momentarily succeeded Shorty Fudd.

So in a way, he hated to see the old telephone number go. He would never learn the outcome of the Fudd picaresque, and the new number meant losing a slew of new friends and acquaintances who had come to know him either as good old Elmer or good old Elmer's assassin — as Shorty Jekyll or Piss Trough Hyde.

CHAPTER ELEVEN

Nocturne in Z

The city of Pine Bluff, which had no bluff and not many pines, was known for three things.

One was its smell. Pine Bluff had a stinky paper mill to the southeast, and to the northwest a federal chemical-and-biological warfare arsenal brewing up beakers of black plague and poison gas. So the city's inhabitants were obliged to check the wind direction to ascertain whether the fetid air on a given day was merely nauseating or potentially lethal.

Pine Bluff's second distinction, perhaps unique, was that it was perfectly bisected by two major railroads, their tracks lying parallel and a block apart in the business district, then fanning out to scissor the residential areas in every direction. There was hardly a viaduct to be seen, so no motorist had ever crossed the city without having to wait for a train. Those who had tried had wound up like Shorty Fudd. The few daredevils who got across the Missouri-Pacific track unstopped and unsmashed were always spotted by the Cotton Belt engineer, who, trained by East German guards at the Berlin Wall, would hurry to cut them off. Then he would throw the brake, and with his train blocking traffic for miles, he and the conductor would swap cannonballing yarns over a friendly Thermos of Nehi. Bruiser once noted in his diary the passing through Pine Bluff of a Cotton Belt freight with eight diesel locomotives, five hundred and two empty boxcars and flatcars and tank-cars, and one red caboose, and he ended the entry with the optimistic note: "Thank God, they seem to be getting shorter."

Pine Bluff probably was best known, though, for its mosquitoes. Without those mosquitoes, W.C. Fields might never have devised his oft-quoted epitaph: "On the whole, I'd rather be in Philadelphia — but not Pine Bluff." Bruiser tended to exaggerate the size and number of Pine Bluff's mosquitoes, but get this: one year while he and Scamp lived there, Pine Bluff thought it had a major blackbird infestation, with one of those gigantic horrid roosts covering a whole section of town. But an alert ornithologist discovered that these "blackbirds" actually were mosquitoes that had flapped up from Bayou Bartholomew and assumed a clever daylight disguise.

It didn't take the Pine Bluff mosquitoes long to knock over Munchkin Manor. One pried loose a window screen and got in one evening shortly after the murder of Shorty Fudd. It wasn't a big Pine Bluff mosquito — only about the size of a hummingbird — but it was shrewd and knew its business. It cased the joint, found itself a bedroom hiding place and started working up an appetite.

Bruiser was late getting home that evening, having labored longer and harder than usual to imbue with Proustian elegance his write-up of a local bowling tourney, and he went right to bed. Scamp saw how exhausted he was, tucked him in, gave him a forehead smack, quietly switched off the light, and went back to the parlor and the late late TV movie. Bruiser closed his eyes and plummeted toward Nod. He would have been there in that immeasurably small amount of time called a quink, but just as he reached the threshold he heard the telltale hum of a Pine Bluff mosquito.

Bruiser was numb all over and actually drunk from fatigue, his faculties already darkly asea, but that hum precipitated another of those hemispheric controversies inside his brain. While the mellowed-out right hemisphere spoke soothingly, "To sleep, perchance to dream," the left hemisphere, command post and supply dump for all the Bruiser phobias, compulsions and eccentricities, heard that drone of mosquito wings and started cranking the air-raid sirens.

Bruiser was too tired to hear them. So Hemisphere Left changed metaphors.

"Go to sleep now," it said, "and that vampire will prowl your flesh and feast on your blood!"

Bruiser squirmed.

Hemisphere Left seized the moment to flash a home movie through Bruiser's mind. In it, Sister Bet took Little Bruiser to a Dracula movie at the old Rex Theater in Sheridan. He was five or six years old, too young to realize that vampires are a literary symbol for utility companies. That movie scared him worse than the rabid dog that bit one of the ringwormy Davis brothers, worse than the Second Coming in his Aunt Laura Bell's gory description of it. It scared him so bad he thought he was going to die.

Frights like that never go very far away; and better than any incantation, a childish association, like that of mosquito beaks and ghoul fangs, can disinter Bela Lugosi and drape a grown man's night with him. Blaise Pascal had Bruiser in mind when he wrote: "We say in vain, He has grown, he has changed; he is also the same."

Hemisphere Right relented with great reluctance and allowed Hemi Left to call the Bruiser faculties back to port. "I know you men are bushed," the latter said, "but we've got the enemy closing in fast on the old boy's starboard ear."

Bruiser couldn't get an exact fix on the hum, so he cocked a bloodshot eye and peered into the Transylvanian darkness above the bed. The drone came nearer, got louder and more distinct, dropped in pitch.

Then it stopped.

Bruiser slapped at his neck.

"Gotcha!"

Hemi Left was undeceived by this Vietnam-style casualty report. "Maintain alert," it ordered.

Heavy seconds passed. The faculties began to drift again, mutinous, sullen. In another instant they would have been beyond recall, unremusterable, but in that instant mosquito music sounded again off the port jowl. It was barely audible but definitely incoming. Bruiser tensed for another slap.

The mosquito anticipated his move and backed away.

"A feint," Hemi Left surmised.

The mosquito moved back almost to the edge of silence, then hovered there — out of reach, out of radar range, dancing on the periphery of Bruiser's awareness with the amused confidence of a veteran taunt.

Hemi Right quoted *Macbeth*: "Trip away, make no stay, meet me all by break of day."

"No! Maintain battle stations!" Hemi Left countered. "That's what he's counting on — that we'll trip away, go to sleep. Fat chance, Needlenose! We can play that old waiting game, too!"

Verily. Many times Bruiser had played this wargame of

nerves and patience. He was no slouch at it, but conceded the mosquito's superiority, with its marvelous sensing equipment that allowed it to Pearl Harbor a colossal host-foe almost with impunity. An engaging game, normally, but Bruiser wasn't up to it this time. His disgruntled faculties drafted an ultimatum: "Either get up, turn on the light, hunt the bastard down and destroy him, or we're gone to Nappy House till cockcrow."

Bruiser plundered all the reserves of his will to raise his leaden bones, fight through the cobwebs to the lamp switch, and turn on the light. He looked around the room and wasn't at all surprised that the mosquito was nowhere to be seen.

The mantis, the moth, the chameleon are amateurs at camouflage compared to the mosquito. The mosquito has a boutique of disguises and can slip into any one of them (and unerringly the right one) in less time than it takes a light bulb filament to illuminate a bedroom. It can blend with the woodgrain of a bedstead, the pattern of a quilt, the delicate shadows of an antimacassar fringe. It can ride invisible on the sweep-second hand of an alarm clock or portray an extension of the coin slot on a piggy bank. Bruiser claimed that once after a nightlong stalk he found and killed a mosquito that had eluded him by spread-eagling over a tiny tear in a window screen in a flawless imitation of the mesh of missing wires. That might have been carrying anthropomorphic hyperbole too far, but Bruiser wasn't particularly rational on this subject.

He found a weathered copy of Albert Schweitzer's *Out of My Life and Thought* to use as a swatter and began his search. He surveyed the ceiling first, then the walls, one by one, inch by inch. Methodically was the only way to do this. He paid special attention to the window, where he found the loosened screen: from the size of the opening he correctly surmised that the intruder was somewhat smaller than a red-shouldered hawk. Next he searched the floor, looking for the teeniest irregularity in the decorative pattern of the linoleum. Since the furniture was hardest to search, with its uneven surfaces and intersecting planes, he saved the furniture for last. He was still reconnoitering the floor, on his hands and knees, when Scamp came in, turned on the light, and said: "What on earth do you think you're doing?"

"Mosquito," he said.

She went to the kitchen and brought back a can of Raid and gave the bedroom a good spraying.

"That's probably a violation of the Geneva Convention," he said.

"You get back in the bed," she told him.

He did, and she turned out the light and exeunted again. How long did he lie there courting sleep? Five minutes? Ten? How could he sleep when Hemi Left was squawking like Audie Murphy: "Imagine! thinking a dose of Raid could kill a Pine Bluff mosquito, reared to mutant maturity on cotton poison, papermill smog and anthrax lab cultures? Dream on, Admiral!"

Bruiser pulled the bedcovers over his face and head, leaving no flesh exposed to attack. He always tried this tactic, in the hope not that he might deny the mosquito but that he might lull Audie just long enough for sleep to gain furtive access. But like most isolationist schemes, this one had never worked, and it didn't work now. After only a few quinks, Hemi Right went berserk: "Hey, god*dam*, this is too much like the *grave!* This is too much like being buried *alive!* Keep your head covered if you want, but I've got to feel the living air, even if it's just with a *toe.*"

"A toe, my foot," sneered Hemi Left. "You know who'll be out there licking its chops waiting for that toe."

Bruiser knew, all right.

And he knew Dr. Freud would be sitting at the end of the bed, saying: "You have read of my studies of Little Hans and the Russian Wolfman, yes? And like them, this is a case of infantile zoophobia, no? Fear of having the toe bit by the mosquito is actually a primal fear of castration. The mosquito is a father figure, and the fear of being eaten by one's father is a common one, as the myth of Kronos suggests."

Bruiser threw back the covers and said some vulgar words.

He lay staring into the dark above his seesaw bed, listening for the hum.

"Why died I not from the womb?" said a voice from neither left nor right. "Why did I not give up the ghost when I came out of the belly? For now should I have lain still and been quiet: I should have *slept!*"

Bruiser recognized the passage from Job and expected Scamp to come back in momentarily and say, "Why don't you just curse God and die?" And maybe the landlord, Shorty's nephew, and Dr. Freud as the comforters. He had a reply ready for them: "My toe looks *nothing* like my scrotum and my daddy don't resemble a Pine Bluff mosquito one bit. This is more like the case of heroic Prometheus, bound to his rock with a giant mosquito tearing at his liver."

The mosquito lingered, lingered, and Bruiser strained to hear the hum. There was no hum. Bruiser imagined Skeeter taking it easy out there in the dark somewhere, on the nightstand or the dresser, sitting back on a chaise lounge of lint, its feet propped up, smoking a very small cigarette. With a sigh, Bruiser switched on the lamp, got up, and started another search. This time he would be thorough. No more delusions of Raid. He inspected the ceiling, walls and floor again; then the window and its curtains; then the dresser, the bureau, the nightstand and the bedcovers.

Nothing.

He dumped the wastebasket on the floor and examined its contents — used tissues, mainly. Then one by one he pulled out the bureau drawers and the dresser drawers and dumped them, rationalizing that a mosquito big enough to pry loose a window screen was certainly capable of opening a drawer and crawling inside. He scrutinized all the spaces between all the rows of bristles in Scamp's hairbrush.

Not a trace.

He thought for a moment that he had run out of places to look. An ordinary mosquito might have crawled through the coin slot into the dark sanctuary of the belly of the pig — but not one large enough to be called a Pine Bluff mosquito. He examined all the knobs, numerals and hands of the clock.

Where else?

Ah!, in his sleepiness, he had neglected the likeliest hideout — the *under*side of the bed. Skeeter could be lolling patiently on a slat. Or hanging inside the spiral of a bedspring as snug as a bat in a cave.

Bruiser was on the floor, on his back, with his head and torso under the bed, probing each bedspring with the digital attentiveness of a proctologist, when Scamp came back into the bedroom.

When she saw the mess he had made — the heaps of clothing, toiletries and trash — she screamed. It wasn't much of a scream, just an understandable eek of dismay, but it was enough to startle Bruiser, who lurched upward, banging his head on the iron bedframe.

The blow sent him swimming among constellations.

He was still cuckoo when Scamp tugged him by the thighs back into the glare of bedroom reality.

She steered him into the kitchen, sat him at the table, and nursed his bruised forehead with a compress.

"I'm glad you're here," he told her.

"I used to spend a lot of time imagining what married life would be like," she said. "I imagined the richer and poorer, the sickness and health, the better and worse. But I never imagined anything like this."

"You wouldn't divorce me?" he said pitifully.

"No, but I got a question if you won't get mad."

"As long as it's not about castration."

"I just wondered if there's any history of insanity in your family that I don't know about."

"You mean just because I was under the bed feeling of those...Ahoy!"

"Ahoy?"

"Did you see it?"

"What?"

"A shadow flitted across the table just now. I saw it out of the corner of my eye."

"You start emptying drawers in here, we might talk castration after all."

"There! Over the refrigerator!"

"What? I don't see anything."

"Quick! Where's Albert?"

"Who?"

"My swatter. Look, it landed on top of the refrigerator. Keep an eye on it while I get Albert. Don't let it get away."

Bruiser dashed into the bedroom and found the book under a scattered heap of empty dresser drawers on the floor. He snatched it up and wheeled back toward the kitchen, but he stopped suddenly. The book had been mashed open at a certain page, and a paragraph on that page hauled him up. This is what it said:

"To the man who is truly ethical all life is sacred, including that which from the human point of view seems lower in the scale. He makes distinctions only as each case comes before him, and under the pressure of necessity, as, for example, when it falls to him to decide which of two lives he must sacrifice in order to preserve the other. But all through this series of decisions he is conscious of acting on subjective grounds and arbitrarily, and knows that he bears the responsibility for the life which is sacrificed. Even if it is only the life of a Pine Bluff mosquito."

"He must still be up there," Scamp said when Bruiser got back to the kitchen. "I didn't see anything move."

"Listen to this," Bruiser said, as though he had completely forgotten the mosquito. He read the passage to her.

"You made up that part about the Pine Bluff mosquito," she said.

"That's beside the point," he said. "The point is, I've been killing these living things all these years without even thinking about what I was doing. You know how many mosquitoes I've killed?"

"How would I know that?"

"Guess."

"A hundred thousand million."

"No, I'm serious."

"You must really hate me."

"Hate you? Why would you say that?"

"I'm here by myself all day with nobody to talk to, and when you finally get home, first you're too tired to talk to me, then you start in about killing bugs."

"I'm sorry," Bruiser said. "What do you want to talk about?"

"I want us to get a pet."

So they talked, sitting there at the kitchen table, about getting a pet.

They talked about getting a pet, and getting a picture to put over the sofa in the parlor, and getting a washing machine and a garbage can. They talked about these and other normal young-married-people topics. They had a good long intimate talk, five minutes at least, and then Scamp was content to ask him: "Okay, how many?"

"Ten thousand four."

"You're making that up, too."

"That's counting the ones I got with the old Flit gun when I was a kid. But most of them I just slapped, mashing the life out of them with the wanton indifference of Samson braining Philistines. Never gave it a thought. But that passage there made me see for the first time that from *their* point of view *I'm* the monster. They probably scare their little larvae by telling them spooky stories about Jack the Slapper and Attila the Hand, slaughtering all their mosquito Beethovens and Madame Curies and Sandra Dees. Look at my forearm here. Skeeter sees that, he don't see an arm; he sees two tiny little Golden Arches, and all he can think is, 'Boy, I'd sure like to stop in there for a strawberry shake.'"

"So what do you plan to do? You can't sleep when one's in the room."

"I don't know. I can either stay awake the rest of my life or spray myself with repellant about two inches thick before I go to bed. Or we could pack up and move. It wouldn't matter where, as long as it was inside the Arctic Circle."

"We might have more room in an igloo."

"I've got some hard thinking to do about this."

"You can't think about anything till you get some sleep."

"I know. I got bags under my eyes I could lay a rope in."

Just then a choppy vibration like the sound of a small helicopter broke the late-night stillness of the apartment, and the whir of mosquito wings raised a small cloud of dust atop the refrigerator. Bruiser impulsively leapt up on a chair and delivered Albert to the scene with a great looping smash. He stood motionless for a few quinks, shocked. Then he slowly turned the book over and found the mosquito corpse silhouetted and stuck fast to the page, blotting out all but a few of the letters in the words *life is sacred*.

"Don't look at me like that," he said guiltily to Scamp. "What's the difference between ten thousand four and ten thousand five. Besides, you said yourself how much I need the sleep."

"I'm going to bed," Scamp said.

"All right, I'm coming, too," Bruiser said, the fatigue lying heavily on him again.

But there was no rest for the weary. The mosquito he killed wasn't the same one. Ten thousand six was waiting for him when he got back in the bed and turned out the light.

CHAPTER TWELVE

Gold Star

One of the few items that Scamp brought into Munchkin Manor that wouldn't fit into the pillow slip slung over Bruiser's shoulder was her spinet piano. She was a gifted pianist, and her playing added a charming touch to the barren little apartment. She put tapestries of sound on the naked apartment walls, warding off the blues with a Chopin nocturne, breaking the tedium with a Schubert *lieder* on a night when TV was all reruns.

Bruiser marveled to watch and hear her play. He thought there was a point at which the music ceased to be sound and became a true picture, an incontestable expression, of who she was. It told him, in a pure voice that didn't have to say, what there was in her that was vital and unique and necessary to keep the world from falling back into chaos. Bruiser envied her that, and thought it might be a way to find out who he really was, too. So one night early on in their marriage, when he was still trying to be the Marcel Proust of the *Pine Bluff Commercial* sports page, he made his bride a proposition. "Tell you what," he said, "you teach me music and I'll teach you to throw a knuckleball like Hoyt Wilhelm's."

Scamp had no nostalgia for the Washington Senators, and she thought the knuckler was a cheap gimmick, like the tackle-eligible pass, but she didn't tell Bruiser that. Nor did she tell him that serious music is a discipline requiring such concentration that his chances of mastering it were about the same as those of Jethro Bodeen of "The Beverly Hillbillies" becoming a brain surgeon. She was always kind to his ego, and protective when his naivete bit off more than it could chew.

She put him off for a time. She had some terrific distractions. But every time he walked by that piano, he looked at it wistfully, the way Michelangelo must have looked at rocks. Beethoven was in there, tempting him like a carnival shill: "Come on, pal, you and me together can fill this parlor with *Fur Elise.*" So he kept after Scamp to instruct him, wearing her down with the nickelodeon plea, "All I want is loving you and music, music, music."

She started him out with some basic music appreciation. She taught him to say Mozart right, and told him the proper name for the overture that he had assumed was "Hi Yo, Silver!" All those showy runs in "Autumn Leaves" didn't necessarily make Roger Williams a virtuoso, and there was more to the Unfinished Symphony than just an elaboration of the Dragnet theme. He had been wrong to think that all of Verdi's stage directions could be translated as, "Okay, everybody get up there and take turns yelling." And only uncouth persons referred to what Robert Merrill did as "yodeling."

Bruiser soaked this stuff up eagerly. He couldn't wait to flaunt his growing store of musical knowledge, so he started dropping musical references into his newspaper sports articles, alternating them with the allusions to the Greek classics:

Johnson lofted the winning jump shot for Dial Junior High with the aggressive yet delicate touch of a roundball Debussy. And: *Linebacker Pertwee blitzed the Trojans with the raging fury of a Rachmaninoff.*

Useful and exciting lore, all right, but it only whetted Bruiser's musical appetite. He wanted to *know* music, not just know about it. He wanted to *make* some of it, instead of being just an appreciative spectator. He nagged Scamp to start his piano lessons.

She distracted him this time by giving him a musical workbook to study and fill out. This workbook introduced him to the language of music. It taught him about clefs, staffs, time signatures, Every Good Boy Does Fine, All Cows Eat Grass, and such as that. One of the pages had a picture of a whole apple and another picture of an apple sliced in half. The text beside those pictures said: "A whole apple is like a whole note. When we cut an apple in two, we have two halves. A half apple is like a half-note. It takes two halves to make an apple.

It takes two half-notes to make a whole note. Color the apples red."

Bruiser read that aloud and said, "I'm not coloring any damn apples."

"I can't give you a gold star on that page, then," Scamp told him.

"A gold star?"

"If you do a page exactly right, I paste a gold star on it. It's like an A-plus. You can take it home and show it to your parents and let them brag on it. Or you could take it to the next ball game you cover, and let the press-box people brag on it. It's really the highest honor a beginner music student can get."

"Oh, all right," Bruiser said, and he began to paw through the crayon box for a red. "I bet Mozart didn't have to color apples when he was starting out."

"He didn't have time," Scamp said. "He was writing concertos when he was four."

"I bet he didn't have to draw the notes to look like apples and then have to color them red."

"He got his ears pulled when he got sassy. Now color those apples while I put supper on."

Bruiser colored the whole apple red, then he colored a burnt umber hole in it and a green worm poking its head out of the hole. And he drew a comic-strip balloon above the worm, with the worm saying, "Ars longa, vita brevis."

While Bruiser colored, the worm talked to him.

"What were you doing when you were four?" the worm said.

"Learning to tie my shoes," Bruiser said.

"That's all?"

"Four wasn't one of my big years."

"If I could live to be four," the worm said, "I'd be the Methuselah of my species. No telling what I might accomplish. You people don't have much respect for life and time. Mozart was more like one of us worms."

Scamp came back in and complimented Bruiser on his coloring and asked about the message in the worm's balloon.

"It means we need to speed this project along," Bruiser said. "If Mozart was writing concertos when he was four, he must've been way ahead of where I am now when he was *two*. At that rate, I'll be past forty when I catch up to where he was at four."

"It was quite a while before he wrote his first symphony, if that's any consolation," Scamp said. "He was eight."

"Was it any good?"

"Compared to what?"

"I don't know. When I was eight, I couldn't make a capital Q. Was this symphony just a bunch of eight-year-old scribbling on his Big Chief tablet, or what?"

"It was a real symphony. Maybe not one of his masterpieces, but I sure couldn't do it."

"That means I'd be *ninety* before I could write even a mediocre symphony."

"Here's a thought," Scamp said. "Bach wrote an average of twenty pages of music every day of his adult life. It'd be hard to get that much done even if it was just gibberish, even if it didn't make any sense. But this was the greatest music in the history of the world. Twenty pages a day. And meantime he was teaching school, playing the organ for church, running around giving concerts for petty nobles to make a little money, and messing around with his wife enough to have twenty kids."

"So what you're saying, no matter what I do in my life, compared to Bach it'll just be a joke."

"You shouldn't look at it like that. You're supposed to be glad he did what he did so we can have his music and enjoy it. He was a person just like us, and there's a little bit of what made him so great in us, too. And he showed us a way to keep in touch with it."

"I wish I *could* think of it like that," Bruiser said. "But I don't want him to have to vouch for me. That's like taking welfare. I want to be able to go through those twenty pages a day of his and say, 'Well, he did okay, but here's the *real* poop.' But instead of that, here I am needing twenty years to catch up with a kid that still dirties his diaper."

Scamp laughed at that but not in an insulting way. "I got to go put the toast in," she said. "Be right back."

"What are we having?"

"Spam and boiled eggs and toast."

That was one of their standard meals during the first years of their marriage. Sometimes they had Vienna sausages and boiled eggs and toast. Sometimes deviled ham and boiled eggs and toast. Sometimes Armour Star chili and boiled eggs and toast. Once a week, when the Magnolia Cafeteria had its all-you-can-eat-for-a-dollar special, they ate out.

"You see why I got to hurry up with the music," Bruiser called to her. "I'm that far behind in music, and music's just one of the things I've got to know. I still got all that Greek crud to master. Then painting and astronomy and auto repair. And that's just *this* year."

"Auto repair?" Scamp called back.

"Yeah, I don't want you thinking, 'Boy, if I'd just stuck with Sonny Gruber, I'd never have to worry about getting the car fixed."

"You can't learn everything," she said.

"I'm aiming to try. If I don't get it all, the most important thing might be in the one place I didn't look. You know that old song, 'All or Nothing at All.' That's how I feel about it."

"Nobody can know it all."

"Aristotle did. And Francis Bacon. The guy on the telephone, Shorty Fudd's buddy, told me about Francis Bacon. Francis Bacon was Shorty's hero. You know how he died? Got pneumonia doing an experiment to see if he could preserve a dead chicken by stuffing it with snow. He was that close to inventing TV dinners — three hundred fifty years ago. He just ran out of time, don't you see?"

"I thought he got hit by a train."

"No, that was Shorty. I'm talking about this Bacon guy now."

"Could you do toaster repair instead of auto repair? One of these toasters is broke."

Bruiser went into the kitchen to look at it.

"See what I mean?" he said. "Somebody wanting to be Aristotle and he don't even know what's wrong with a toaster. He can't fix a bed. Colors apples. Listen, Scamp, if that brat could write a concerto at four, I know damn well I can learn to play the Blue Danube in a week."

Knowing better, she let him take the honored place at the piano after supper. "Just show me some of the preliminaries," he said, "and this time next week I'll have Liberace offering me bribes."

She left him alone a while, to monkey with the Strauss while she washed the dishes. She looked in on him a time or two, watching him laboriously repeat his Every Good Boy Does Fine on each note. Ignoring the left hand and pedals, he one-fingered only the melody line but managed to transform the Blue Danube into a mongrelization of "The Stars and

Stripes Forever" and "The Daring Young Man on the Flying Trapeze." He put poor gentle Strauss through unspeakable torment for nearly an hour before conceding. "All right," he said to Scamp, "maybe we ought to try it your way."

She put him to work on "Old McDonald Had a Farm" in the Schaum Green Book, the traditional piano-student primer and the perennial leading cause of institutionalization, attempted suicide, and child abuse among piano teachers. After what seemed an eternity, she tried, through clenched teeth, to give him a bit of encouragement, telling him that his timing on the "here a cluck, there a cluck, everywhere a cluck cluck" was pretty good, and that they could wait until the next lesson to concern themselves with the triviality of hitting an occasional right note.

Bruiser hung in there against Old McDonald through three bruising lessons. He never yielded an inch. But Scamp finally interceded. "We can do one of two things," she said. "Either skip over to the next piece or call the little guys in the white coats."

"I think I've got the gist of this one anyway," Bruiser said. "I'll come back and mop up on it after I've perfected my technique."

The next piece was one named "Hot Dog Stand." Scamp got through forty-seven of his stabs at it. In the middle of the forty-eighth, she politely excused herself. "I need to take a walk around the block," she said. "If I never come back, I think you'll know why."

It was several days before she was able to compose herself enough to supervise another lesson. They didn't look at "Hot Dog Stand," and avoided mention of it, moving directly to a ditty titled "The Riddle."

Before trying to play it, Bruiser read the words aloud:

Poets and Pigs! Poets and Pigs!
What is the diff'rence? Think!
Poets all have a pen and ink!
Pigs all have a pen and oink!

He read them through a second time, slowly, a troubled look creasing his brow.

"What's going on here?" he said.

"That's what I've been wondering since we started," Scamp said.

"No, listen to this," he said, reading the words out loud again. "Can you believe that? Comparing Keats to some nasty old hog out here beside the road. Saying the difference between them is barely worth mentioning. I'm not sitting still for propaganda like this, Scamp."

"Just concentrate on the music. The words in this case don't matter."

"Don't *matter!*"

"I mean you're trying to learn to play the piano, not be a poetry critic. At least I *thought* that's what you were doing."

"This just won't *do*," Bruiser said. "Somebody's got to tell this Nazi composer where to get off. Maybe he thought it was a cute little joke, but little *kids* are studying this book, and he's planting an evil seed here. Let him get away with it and ten years from now some high school English teacher will say 'John Milton' and a dozen teenagers around the room will automatically oink."

"Just go on the the next page then."

"All right, but these Schaum people are going to hear from me about this. Poets and pigs! Next they'll be doing 'Playwrights and Slugs.' Or 'Sportswriters and Lice.'"

"What's the next piece?"

"'Donkey Party.'"

"Does it slander anybody?"

"It might be a fable about one of the Democratic conventions. But nothing vicious like 'Poets and Pigs.' I guess you think I'm being silly."

"I wouldn't call anybody silly who keeps a lifetime body count of all the mosquitoes he's killed."

"It's the same principle. Brainwash a kid to think of poets as pigs, it's easy to make him think of black people as apes or Jews as vermin, and so forth. But take somebody that worries about the morality of slapping a mosquito, he won't be a rope carrier for the Klan or the camp doctor at Dachau. You see what I mean?"

"You threatened to kill Shorty's nephew."

"That was different. I got nothing against *scaring* a mosquito."

"Maybe this composer *likes* pigs. Maybe he thinks pigs are sensational. Maybe comparing poets to them was the highest compliment to poets he could think of."

Bruiser considered that.

"No," he said. "This guy had it in for poets. You can read

between the lines and tell that."

"There's a cute little pig on 'Green Acres.'"

"Poets aren't supposed to be cute. Calling them cute is just another way of putting them down so the tyrants can take over."

"So if I think Arnold the Pig is cute, I'm in favor of dictatorship?"

"How much of a jump is it from Arnold the Pig to Matthew Arnold and from cute to frivolous? And from there, dictatorship is right around the corner."

"You want to see what violence you can perpetrate on 'Donkey Party' now?"

He perpetrated about forty-five minutes' worth. Then he put his head down on the keyboard and said ruefully: "I'm not doing so hot with the music, am I?"

"I told you it takes time," she said. "A year from now you'll be doing great."

"But I won't be playing 'Summertime' the way you do. The way you play it makes me want to run out and find some little darkie and say, 'Don't worry, chile, everything's going to be all right now.' How long till I can do that?"

"Depends on how much you're willing to practice."

"If I could play 'Clair De Lune' the way you do, I'd be satisfied."

"If you work at it, you can."

"Hell, I'm working at 'Donkey Party.' I'm sweating *blood* over 'Donkey Party.' And it sounds like a donkey party, too. It sounds like a bunch of drunk donkeys playing Stomp the Piano."

"You just want to quit, then?"

"No, I don't want to just quit."

"Try it one more time and we'll let you go back and mop up on Old McDonald."

"How'll I ever get to 'Clair De Lune' if I have to go back and start over with Old McDonald every time? That's like being sent down to the minors every week. Or being sent back to Little League every week. Can you give me a rough idea how long before I can do a first-rate 'Clair De Lune'?"

"Maybe two or three years. If you really practice."

"Don't they have something like the Evelyn Wood speed reading course for piano players?"

"Not that I know of."

"Maybe I ought to do the banjo."

"Maybe so."

"No, the damn banjo never civilized anybody. How much practice are you talking about?"

"Three hours a day, maybe. You said first-class; it'll take that much."

"Wouldn't leave me time for all the other stuff I got to learn."

Scamp shrugged.

"Even if I said okay, you know what would happen," he said. "It'd be like a diet. I'd do it for a month, then something would come up and I'd never get back to it. And a few years from now, instead of 'Clair De Lune,' I'd be doing Chopsticks. We'd go to a party and when it got boring, I'd wind up at the piano playing Chopsticks. Everybody would clap and say, "Hey, that was great; do something else.' And I'd get real depressed because I wouldn't *know* anything else.

"And I already know the painting will work out the same way. My masterpiece will be a velvet matador. And auto repairs — I might as well face it: Sonny Gruber I'm not. I could change five hundred oil pumps and I'd still be like my brother-in-law. Digs around under the hood till he gets grease in his hair and up his nose, and bloodies up two knuckles, and the upshot every time is to make the garage mechanic's job about three times as hard. And these Greek classics — it might be four or five *years* before I completely master them."

"You did get a gold star on your apple, though," Scamp said.

Bruiser thought about that. "I'll always have that star, won't I?"he said.

"Darn right," Scamp said. "Some people go through their whole life and never get one."

"You're too good to me, Scamp."

"True."

"I mean it."

"We all need somebody to remind us once in a while of our gold star," she said, and it was one of the best things he ever heard anybody say. It had her music in it.

Thus was Keyboard Bruiser stillborn, somewhere between the poets and pigs, on the road to ei-ei-o. He had learned to say Vagner and Hahndel, to know the difference between a mazurka and a Polish pickle; but he would never hear the Bruiser music, the song of his incontestable self. And he wore that gold star ever after as a kind of Purple Heart over a bruise that never did completely heal.

CHAPTER THIRTEEN

Armadillo Burnout

Bruiser realized ere long that sportswriting was not his calling. It affected him badly. He began to think in sporting metaphors, like a Republican president. He would come home from work in the evening and Scamp would ask how his day had been and he would say:

"Well, I gave it a hundred ten per cent out there. You can't ask for more than that. I don't have the talent and experience of some reporters but I try to make up for it with discipline and hard work. Working on the fundamentals, you know. I really stress execution, you know. You know?"

Gene Foreman, the managing editor who was well known throughout the world of journalism, noticed this creeping affliction and took pity. He changed Bruiser's assignment from sportswriting to what was called feature writing.

Bruiser was thrilled. The new assignment meant more prestige and a five-dollar-a-week raise. Bruiser was actually more thrilled about the raise than the prestige; the raise would allow him and Scamp to buy a wall picture at the discount store to hang over the nail holes in the plaster above the Munchkin Manor parlor sofa. The fruits of success are sweet indeed.

They bought a print showing a Paris streetcorner in the rain. It was a sad scene, green and black and depressing, and Bruiser and Scamp both hated it but each thought the other liked it or saw some redeeming artistic quality in it, so they kept it around for seven unnecessary years and rejoiced when it was damaged beyond repair by a moving company. The mover said nobody had ever congratulated him before for destroying their home furnishings.

The first "feature" event that Bruiser was sent to limn was the annual turtle derby in the nearby small town of Gould. Gould was named for Jay Gould, but Arkansas people pronounced it like ghoul, and that pronunciation had a ring of truth. Henry Morton Stanley, who found Dr. Livingstone later on, once lived near Gould, but otherwise, in the parochial argot, Gould had sort of sucked hind titty.

A turtle derby is something like a frog-jumping contest, only the contestants are turtles instead of frogs and they crawl rather than hop. They crawl when they feel like it, that is — and that's seldom. At Gould, the contestant turtles were placed in the center of a large chalk-drawn circle, and the first to crawl out of the circle was declared the winner. Human beings stood around the circle and cheered. Sometimes they cheered for the better part of a day, waiting for one of the turtles to move. These humans cared more about winning the turtle derby than the turtles did. The turtles didn't care *any*thing about it, insofar as Bruiser could see. They had no reason to. The winning turtle didn't get the trophy or his picture in the paper — his human sponsor did. But even if the turtle *had* got to keep the trophy and *had* been photographed in a triumphant pose, it's doubtful he would have exerted himself to win this derby. He might have started out strong, but after a few inches he would have stopped for a smoke, lingering there far short of the finish line to reminisce about old friends and old times and to hum all the verses of *Zippedy Doo Dah* two or three hundred times. That's just the way turtles are.

The glory of winning meant more to the human turtle-sponsors than the trophy. A human in Gould, Arkansas, might go through his whole life and never get his picture in the newspaper but twice: once when he got married, and once when he sponsored the winning turtle in the Gould Turtle Derby. So the derby was no inconsequential thing. And Bruiser tried to keep that in mind when, two years in a row, he wrote his feature article about the human sponsor of the winning turtle. The second year's article was shorter. That wasn't because the subject was less interesting or deserving; it was because, after the first time, Bruiser found that no matter how hard he tried he just couldn't give much of a rat's ass about racing turtles or the people who raced them.

He came to feel the same way about the tomatoes at the annual tomato festival at Warren, the armadillos at the annual armadillo barbecue at Hamburg, the ducks at the annual duck-calling contest at Stuttgart, the raccoons at the annual Gillett Coon Supper. Here's what he thought: he probably had no more than nineteen thousand days left to live, and it wasn't right to squander one of those precious days trying to compose a new feature-writer tribute to a tomato or a goddam duck.

This time, Well-Known Managing Editor Gene Foreman did not sympathize.

"That tomato pays your salary," Gene said. "It bought you that picture over the sofa in your parlor. There are eight hundred million Chinese who don't have any picture at all over their sofas, you know. So quit complaining."

Gene talked tough like that, but underneath he was an old softie. It hurt him to see anyone suffering from armadillo burnout. So after a year or two he gave Bruiser *another* five-dollar raise, which made possible a much-needed lube job and new wiper blade for the Phantom Rickshaw, and changed his assignment again. Bruiser would do his write-ups hereafter on politicians and their campaigns.

This assignment introduced Bruiser, who knew the Greeks pretty well by now, to the Romans. At one time or another, just about all the politicians Bruiser listened to and wrote about made a speech with this title: Why Rome Fell. It fell because of moral decay and welfare chiselers and smoking marijuana and some other historically verifiable reasons, they said. And the United States was following the same path. So people better vote for them or it would be the Visigoths and Huns and hippies and jigaboos all over again.

Bruiser never could adapt to the high standards of political journalism. Instead of being objective or fair, he wanted to lay it on the line. He wanted, in Mencken's phrase, to shout and flap his arms. Here's an example: one time Gene Foreman sent Bruiser to hear a politician make a speech in the town of Hot Springs. When Bruiser returned, he told Gene: "I'm sorry but I can't write an article about that. The man is obviously deranged and he had nothing original or intelligent to say."

Gene sighed and said: "People buy this newspaper to find out what's going on. So write me an article about what the man said, not what you think of what he said. Either that or you can go back to armadillos; I don't care what you say about armadillos."

Bruiser didn't feel quite right about it, but he tried to follow orders. Here's what he wrote:

Richard Nixon, the former vice president, made a speech at Hot Springs Saturday. He thinks he's got a chance to be the next president of the United States. Ha, ha.

This was not what Gene had in mind, either, and Bruiser might have been in real occupational trouble here if Ed Freeman, in the manner of the Great Travis Shellnut, hadn't come to his rescue. Ed, you'll recall, was one of the owners of the newspaper — the one who had introduced Bruiser to the Greeks. And now, as if in league with those slapstick Olympians, he proposed to make Bruiser the paper's opinion writer, its editorial man.

Bruiser was suspicious at first. He did not, in the editorial writer's parlance, think unhighly of himself, but he was of an age when he should have been going to pep rallies and making D's in the required social science courses, and his knowledge of world affairs had roughly the same sophistication and profundity as *Cracked* magazine's or the Harvard School of Government's. He didn't know at the time that his notions on contemporary events were no more stupid than anyone else's, and actually were less offensive than most, tempered as they were by genuine intellectual humility, and unpolluted yet by all the careerist and ideological sludge. But in the merciless serial indictment of cold print, his opinions turned out to be a muddle, a chaos; there was not yet inside him a clearly defined thinker to give them coherence and styling. He had not yet found his "voice."

This is a fairly common handicap among writers who haven't written much — and alas among many who have — and it might have been more pronounced in Bruiser because he had read so little and thus had such scant knowledge of the language and of the wonders its masters could make it perform. Because he lacked a distinctive voice of his own, Bruiser tended to rant in a style imitating that of whoever he was reading. His Dos Passos diatribes against the state Game and Fish Commission might have been memorable if they hadn't been incomprehensible, and it just wasn't every effective to use an e.e. cummings approach to try to shame some neighborliness into the Klan.

But he did the best he knew how. From his perch there in

the cottonpatch and germ-warfare wastes of the Arkansas delta, Bruiser passed daily judgment on the powers and principalities. He gave Charles DeGaulle and Mao Tse-Tung so much good advice that it was pitiful. He was constantly reminding Sukarno or somebody that those who didn't know Santayana were doomed to repeat him. He assessed the agony of India in just about every way that it could have been assessed.

"How about if we give India a breather," Ed Freeman would say occasionally, "and say something about the corruption down at City Hall?"

"I know what you mean," Bruiser would say. And he *did* know. He knew how much all the bean farmers down at Star City and all the muffler shop guys there in Pine Bluff cared about his assessments of the agony of India. But there was something of missionary work in editorial writing – something that required treating of India's agony just as feature writing had required treating of armadillos; just as sportswriting had required lionizing imbeciles. Assessing India's plight was just one of those ongoing jobs that somebody had to do, and the worst part of it was that India didn't appreciate it any more than the Star City bean men did.

Bruiser held forth as the *Commerical*'s editorial man for a little more than a year, and if all his afghani forays, his gibes at Franco, his tributes to veterans and spring, were something less than an inspiration to Pine Bluff's geopolitical illuminati, they meant a great deal to him. They allowed him to search diligently and pretty much continuously for that "voice," for that evolving other inside himself whose emergence or coalescence would bring order to the Bruiser chaos. That voice was the one that would tell him who he was and what he must do with his life.

Political writer Bruiser did come across one politician who said some original things. This politician's name was Winthrop Rockefeller. He was the black sheep of John D.'s grandsons, and his image-conscious brothers exiled him to Arkansas after his sensational divorce from Bobo Sears. He bought himself a mountain in Arkansas and raised cows on it. Toward the end of his life, he ran for governor of the state four times and got elected twice. He was the worst public speaker ever elected to public office in Arkansas or anywhere else. But people voted for him because they assumed he was so rich he wouldn't need to be crooked.

Winthrop was a big, awkward man who wore a cowboy hat and boots. Every day he smoked five packs of rolled death called Picayune cigarettes and drank a couple of quarts of gin. The gin probably helped him get his tang tonguled up whenever he went to make a campaign speech.

"And when that happened," he said in one of those speeches, discussing a surprising occurrence, "you could have knocked me over with a fine-toothed comb."

Winthrop's army of aides-de-camp and hangers-on called him by a familiar shortened form of his first name, Win. And it happened that he made one of his most famous campaign speeches in an Arkansas town named Wynne, which was pronounced the same way. Win speaking at Wynne.

He got to Wynne after a long hot day of campaigning in dozens of small delta towns, all of which looked pretty much the same to him, especially after he got into that second quart of gin. So he was tired and a little snockered when he wobbled up to the microphone there in the high school football stadium at Wynne, where a great throng had gathered at dusk to hear him speak. He looked out over the great cheering multitude, and, heaving a deep breath to steady himself, said into the microphone:

"Boy, it's great to be with you tonight here at..."

He suddenly realized that he didn't know which town he was in. There had been so many that day.

So he started again. "Boy, it's great to be with you tonight here at..."

He still couldn't recall. So the campaign aide who had introduced him and had subsequently taken a seat on the platform gave him a stage whisper: "Wynne!"

Winthrop tried again.

"Boy, it's great to be with you tonight here at..."

The aide whispered louder and more urgently: "Wynne! Wynne!"

Win tried once more and when he still couldn't come up with the town's name, several other embarrassed aides on and around the platform took up the desperate whisper: "Wynne! Wynne! Wynne!"

They finally got his attention, and he heard what they were saying, but he only glowered at them. And not bothering to cover the open mike, he told them sternly:

"Goddam it, I know my *name*. Tell me where I *am*!"

Winthrop once brought R. Buckminster Fuller, the inventor of the geodesic dome, down to Arkansas to speak to a distinguished gathering. Like most of Fuller's acquaintances, Winthrop called him Bucky.

Winthrop made the introductory speech, and got flustered as usual. He concluded by saying, "Ladies and gentlemen, it's my privilege to present to you a great man, Mr. Fucky Buller."

Realizing the mistake, he quickly corrected himself: "Oh, you know what I mean — Bull Fucker!"

A PATERNITY SUITE

THREE POP SELECTIONS:

The Music of Creation
D.J.
Trick or Treat

CHAPTER FOURTEEN

The Music of Creation

His assignment was to drive that Friday afternoon the forty miles from Pine Bluff to Little Rock, where he would catch a small chartered press plane that would ferry him to Huntsville, high in the Ozarks, for an evening Lincoln's Birthday political rally honoring Winthrop Rockefeller. After the rally, he would return from the hills to the delta, and, sometime before the sunrise deadline, produce a smartly written account of the rally for the Saturday edition of the Pine Bluff newspaper.

Bruiser dreaded the trip. He wasn't afraid of flying, exactly — having experienced a few years before that lugubrious journey to Memphis in the freezing cargo hold of a Navy transport plane, he considered himself an old hand at flying — but recent disclosures (at least they were recent to him) about midair emergencies had considerably darkened his outlook on the wonders of mechanical flight. There had been a row of parachutes along the wall of that Navy plane, and Bruiser had assumed them to be in working order, even though a certain musty air of abandonment emanated from them, hinting of rotting canvas and disintegrating ripcord. He had supposed from that experience that *all* planes had parachutes and permitted their passengers to strap themselves in and take their chances by leaping into the void in certain extreme instances of high-altitude crackup and conkout. But a worldly-wise colleague had recently informed him — rather blithely, Bruiser thought — that such was not the case. Bruiser was flabbergasted.

"What are you supposed to do up there?" he said. "Just call a huddle and everybody sing 'Nearer My God to Thee'?"

"I know what I'd do," his colleague said with a shrug. "Drink me about twenty bottles of airline liquor — in other words, about one good belt — and grab me a stewardess and ravish her all the way down. What a climax!"

"I can't be that say la vee about it," Bruiser said, using the French to stress his outrage. It was unnatural enough, he thought, to be bopping around the ether on somebody else's artificial wings; but to be condemned there, without warning and without recourse or appeal, just wasn't right or reasonable. He grew moody thinking about that, more so when he realized that, even had he been the type to grandstand with meteoric debauch his crossing into campground, a chartered flight this small wouldn't have a stewardess.

He also dreaded the trip because Scamp was due to deliver at any time, and he didn't want her to be alone for the big event.

But he didn't want to be unemployed, either, so he made the drive to Little Rock by way of Sheridan, leaving his roly-poly bride there with family, promising to pick her up bright and early on the morrow. He motored on to Little Rock alone, pondering the prospect that he would soon be a father for the second time.

Father Bruiser: it seemed to him that he was getting ahead of himself here somehow; he was reproducing without having first produced. Caterpillar bringing forth caterpillar without butterfly having flown. Maybe the reproduction was the production, he thought; maybe that was all that was expected and even wanted of him, to serve as momentary custodian of the helix, to contribute to the continuation of the old and unfinished experiment, and then to get on out of the way. Maybe that was all there was to it, and the rest was just self-indulgence; the rest was just poetry; the rest was just superfluous energy which, in the process of burning itself off, produced the curious and futile vapor of self-awareness. Reproduction as an act of unconscious despair.

This was Bruiser being metaphysical. He had learned that in college. It didn't portend a carefree flight to Huntsville.

The little airplane got away from Little Rock smoothly, but just as it reached cruising altitude it collided head-on with a winter storm moving down through Arkansas from the north. The storm played some mumbledepeg and blanket-toss with it, and Bruiser learned what life must be like for a pinball. Then it caught a down-draft, and the bottom fell out. The plane dropped a thousand feet in less time than it took Bruiser to gulp. His eardrums, caught off guard, collapsed under the sudden heavy air pressure. He felt his head mashed oblong, into an unwilling Modigliani, and he screamed.

Or he *thought* he screamed.

He went through the motions of screaming, but the cabin of the airplane remained as silent as death.

He tried again, but the only sound was a distant ominous cracking, like the eerie crunch of renegade ice floes in the Arctic night.

The Johnny Belinda nightmare had been in Bruiser's stable of dreams since he was yea-high — the scream sticking in the throat in a time of great peril or horror — and it seemed now to have escaped into waking reality. Only when the three other reporters who had been shoehorned into the plane began to try to subdue and calm him did Bruiser realize that his screams had been audible after all.

To everyone but himself.

He wasn't mute; he was *deaf.*

The plane bored through the storm and landed on a mountain runway glazed with sleet, skidding to a stop in a field of goldenrod after a suspenseful slide that caused Bruiser to whap his snoot on the seat in front of him. The pilot had a hand towel and Bruiser used that to catch the nosebleed, but there was no help for the godawful pain in his ears or for the spooky silence that made him feel like a marooned frogman or a self-conscious asteroid. He was so distracted as he deplaned that he didn't notice the high-altitude cold. The temperature behind the storm had sunk to near Farenheit zero. He'd brought no overcoat, of course, and Nature in her beneficience might have gone on and put him out of his misery, like one of Jack London's klondike klutzes, had not one of the world's richest men seen him, pitied him, and draped his own camel's hair jacket over the rime forming on the Bruiser shoulders.

Only the churlish gods or Horatio Alger could have authored such melodrama, but Bruiser had accepted that a certain Shorty Fudd pathos was going to dog his life, and he valiantly sat through the political festivities and oratory with a bloody towel under his nose and tears of brutal pain on his cheeks, dutifully scribbling quotations for his newspaper dispatch — quotations which he gathered by an arduous process of trying diligently to read dignitaries' lips.

It was after midnight when the plane got back to Little Rock. Bruiser was still deaf, still hurting, still bleeding from time to time. And exhausted. He walked to the airport parking lot in a bathysphere of unhearing, with the ghostly tread of an Iroquois scout or the Great Sky Bear. He did two hundred twenty nine dollars worth of damage to the engine of his car by trying to start it after it had already started. He was afraid to drive home to Pine Bluff because that forty-mile stretch of highway was notoriously dangerous even in good weather in the daytime, and he was so disoriented by the utter silence which enveloped him that he had no way of knowing from one moment to the next if he was awake or asleep. Strange thoughts seeped up through the midnight silence as he drove along: "Somebody ought to invent a parachute that you wear in a *car*."

It was two o'clock when he got to Pine Bluff. He typed up his account of the political rally in the deepest mental fog to enwreath a working writer since DeQuincey detoxed. It was the most complimentary political report he ever made, and that was due to his discovery that politicians aren't nearly so obnoxious when one doesn't hear what they're saying. Bruiser even wondered if a mute politics, shorn of rhetoric, might not be the silent answer to the great questions which the world doesn't know how to ask. A voiceless politician might start a war, but he would be hard put to sustain one. He would have a devil of a time raising a mob. His would cease to be the amusement politics of monkeys and become the watchful politics of cats. People would have to look at him and pay attention to know what he was saying, and then they would know exactly, and that would make a difference. Lincoln might have prospered as a voiceless politician, but Bruiser couldn't think of anyone else.

At four in the morning, he finished the write-up and left the newspaper office. He had no trouble starting the car this time, thanks to the violent vibrations of the damaged engine, but he nearly got Shortied by a Cotton Belt freight because he didn't hear the DDR engineer rushing to block the intersection. The pain in his ears was his sole assurance that he wasn't just a bad idea thought up and then banished by Edgar Allan Poe, or a gothic shadow, conjured by dyspepsia from flat ale, on the perimeter of one of Blake's visions or Kafka's dreams. He was so tired and crazy that he nearly wrecked the car again as he turned on to his home street, mistaking the line of conifers there for a procession of giant hooded monks who were about to step on him. But his ears kept jabbing him back to mortal awareness. They got him home, undressed him, and heaved the tonnage of his granite flesh into the sailing ship of bed. But then they kept him awake.

He lay in a conscious coma, hearing ancient and ethereal sounds carom along passageways and searoutes and starlanes in his brain — pings and gronks that might have been reptilian residue barnacled on the Bruiser genes, screes and whings that might have been inscribed during the primordial chaos on the drifting dust. Deaf people hear, he discovered, but what they hear is the random coded music of the creation, the song of electrons and microbes, the infinitesimal psalm of the quark.

"Who are you?" they asked Bruiser. "What mission did you call us together to perform?"

Bruiser could not answer them. He was wandering voiceless inside the enormous amorphous mass of himself, and didn't know.

Among all those alien silhouettes and fossils of sound was one that was remotely familiar. It was familiar enough to invite analogy: it was like the faint distant sound of a telephone ringing. Maybe the telephone in the vacant house four doors down at the end of the street. Or a telephone that Bruiser only remembered hearing — when he was still Little Bruiser or Baby Bruiser or Foetal Bruiser, listening through the wall of a womb.

It didn't seem unusual to him that he would hallucinate the faraway ring of a telephone. Nothing seemed unusual in that state where there was no usual. Other phantom sounds soon joined that of the telephone — a muffled thumping, like the flutter of a lover's heart; the suggestion of a commotion just beyond hearing, with a vague human quality about it, like the spectral cries and whispers said to trouble the air betimes in the Roman catacombs and in the ruins of Pompeii; and the unmistakable tinkle of breaking glass.

Glass?

A hand gripped Bruiser's shoulder and he jumped straight up out of the bed.

The hand continued to hold him, and the glare of a flashlight filled his eyes. Then the light moved, and the hand moved, and the lamp on the table beside the bed illuminated.

Bruiser couldn't hear a thing, and there was a moment of terror before he was able to comprehend what he saw.

What he saw was his next-door neighbor, Mr. Browning, robed and slippered, standing beside the bed moving his lips much too rapidly to read.

"What is it? What is it? Ho! Yawk! Halloo! Halloo!"

Bruiser couldn't hear himself saying any of those things which Mr. Browning told him later that he said, and said with the volume of a sonic boom. Bruiser only knew that he was trying to ask what was the matter, having assumed from Mr. Browning's anxious expression — and from his unlikely presence at five a.m. — that something was afoot.

"Lord god, man, we thought you were dead!" Mr. Browning was saying. "You didn't answer the phone and I nearly beat the door down. Sorry I had to break the window but it was the only way I knew to get in."

"What? What is it? Halloo! Halloo!"

Doing his best to read Mr. Browning's fast-moving lips, Bruiser concluded that the house must be on fire.

"Let's get out of here! Yike! Ho! Gronk de frong! Saarg!"

(Bruiser had no idea, when Mr. Browning told him of them later, what those last two exclamations meant. Possibly what he intended to say was, "Help! Help!" Or, "Thanks for the warning, Mr. B., but now it's every man for himself.")

By employing some anthropoid gestures and other Cro-Magnon communicative techniques, Bruiser eventually got it across to Mr. B. that he was deaf, and Mr. B. got it across to him that Scamp had gone into labor over at Sheridan and wanted him to get over there pronto.

Bruiser never could remember afterward how he got to Sheridan. Maybe the relentless pain in his ears really was the clutch of a guardian angel, mercy's seraphim, who threaded the car over that flumppy old highway past all those beckoning borrow pits and utility poles like goliath hitchhikers. He knew only that for a time night's whirling effluvium held him once more, and that the giant suck of Sheridan drew him like a black hole and deposited him like driftwood at the proper door.

And then he was in the back seat of another car, holding Scamp, whose groans he couldn't hear as someone else drove them madly toward the delivery room at St. Vincent's Infirmary in Little Rock.

They reached the hospital at 6:29 a.m. and Bruiser Jr. entered the world at 6:42.

Kindly old Dr. Rogers was a man of few words. His lips were easy to read. "A boy. Mother and baby both fine."

Uncertain where to go next, unsure where he was, Bruiser began wandering down a white tiled hallway in the dipsydoodle fashion of an astronaut walking in space.

His son had just had such a passage, he thought.

His son didn't know yet what it meant to be a son, and Bruiser didn't know yet what it meant to be a son *or* father.

There were sounds in this corridor that nobody else heard, and one of them was the distant voice of Isaiah: "For unto you a child is born; unto you a son is given. And his name shall be called..."

Never mind the name that would be put on him for the sake of convenience for the time being. The true name — the one that would attest his true existence — would seek him out some day, would move in for good, would remember him to the world after he was gone.

Bruiser was still awaiting his own true name — a name that would encompass son, brother, husband, friend, scribbler, yearner, dreamer, and now father and father again.

As the angel dragged him along that corridor, Bruiser thought about the importance of true names. But his thoughts were agglutinated by fatigue, loose ends converging into a lento commedia dell'arte. When he saw an empty armchair in a waiting room off to the side, he literally fainted into it.

His angel, in a three-cornered hat, came by a short time later and tucked around him the bloodstained camel's-hair coat that he had forgot to give back to the man named Rockefeller.

CHAPTER FIFTEEN

D.J.

Bruiser's father was nothing like Ward Cleaver or Ozzie Nelson. Daddy Joe was from the old benign-neglect school of fatherhood. He wasn't one to let his head be turned very much or very often by either the joys or tribulations of the institution, because it was only rarely that he remembered to remember that he *was* a father. He fertilized the ova and earned the grocery money, and left the detail work of child-rearing to Polly.

That's not to say that Daddy Joe disliked children or treated them badly. He talked to his children sometimes, and played with them, but in the same way that a man might talk to or play with a pet. His play was a form of teasing that put him in the role of ogre. He would growl at youngsters, or jump at them from behind doors, or chase them around the front-yard washpot, telling them that if he caught them he was going to skin their heads, or tan their hides, or give them to the boog-erman, or put them to work at some odious chore — cleaning out the well, or helping him roof the high gable of the house. Some of his children and grandchildren (and neighbors' children and relatives' children — they were all the same to him) knew instinctively that this was his harmless idea of amuse-ment, and they either shared or endured the good time he was having at their expense. But some of them — the Original Gopher Wells, for instance — were so terrified by his horseplay that they would run off to the woods or climb the closest tall tree whenever they saw him coming.

That cartoon relationship was the only kind he ever established with children because he just wasn't quite able to think of children as people. He seemed to think of them as apprentice people. Or potential people. Because of that, he couldn't keep their names straight, and differences of gender were usually lost on him. Thus when his own offspring were small, he called them all "Buck" except on those infrequent occasions when he noticed that one of them was a girl, and he would call her "Sis." There were four Bucks and three Sisses. And when the next generation came along, grandsons and granddaughters alike were Buck. When he had to call one of them by name, he would take a guess, and it was seldom right but sometimes close — Carolyn for Karen, Jerry for Gary, Bryant for Brian. He called Bruiser's children — daughter Scampette and son Bruiser Jr. — "the boys."

Names were an unnecessarily complicated business generally, to his thinking, and he simplified fancy or trendy names by changing them to solid old-fashioned ones. His favorite baseball player was Sam Musial. He also liked Jill Hodges, whom he must have thought was an awfully big old gal.

Once children reached a certain age or size or stage of development, though — once they emerged from the muppet mass and became recognizable people — Daddy Joe accepted them as peers and thought the world of them. It was as though he had shepherded them through some secret rite of passage that nobody but him knew about. One day, there they were, people, and he was just as proud of them as could be. He seemed to get more satisfaction from his grown children's accomplishments than they did, even though their various military and corporate and artistic pursuits were only a grand mystery to him, as life itself was.

Daddy Joe died before Bruiser matured enough to fully appreciate him. Cancer of the spine killed him with merciful quickness. He suffered only a few months.

He died in the front bedroom of the sagging frame house that he had built with his own hands from cadged lumber and hoarded nails in the middle of the Great Depression. Polly and Dr. Jack were in the bedroom with him during the last hour, while the four Bucks and three Sisses sat around the living room, waiting in a hush of resignation.

When Dr. Jack came out of the bedroom and shook his head as a way of saying it was over, Bruiser got up from the sofa and went out to the front porch. It had been raining when he arrived at the home place that morning, but now the sun was out and the clouds had scattered to reveal a bright blue April afternoon.

Bruiser stood on the porch a while, looking out over all the automobiles in the yard and the yellow broomsedge beyond. Then, thrusting his hands into his pants pockets to keep them from shaking fists at the sky, he set out walking.

He walked up to the fishing pond that Daddy Joe had built just over the hill on the back side of the home place soon after his retirement from the sawmill seven years earlier. Bruiser walked up there to be alone and to think about his father.

On such days as this one was, retired Daddy Joe would go out into the back yard after breakfast, hoe up some red wigglers, drive up the hill to the pond in that ramshackle pickup that had so embarrassed Adolescent Bruiser, and do a little fishing and a lot of work. Only he didn't consider the work work. Not even when it consisted of hard labor — grubbing stumps or warring against the advance of the honeysuckle and sawbriars or clearing beggarlice and sassafras snags with a slingblade. How could it be work when he was doing exactly what he wanted to be doing, and pretty much what he had waited all his life to be doing?

And particularly on such days as this one was, in April, when the hill's natural cycles again were in the resurrection stage, and he could take time to consider the metamorphosis of the polliwogs or the new leaves on the walnut and red-haw trees, which had begun to spread the season's first deciduous shade across the shallow water where the bass spawned.

The sky at the pond had been scrubbed clean by the rain, and a flotilla of big white clouds made a majestic backdrop for the high buzzard whorls. The cardinals and meadowlarks were singing as if nothing had happened, and the bluejays were heckling Janice's calico cat. The blue herons and wood ducks were gone but the crows were patrolling their territorial border along the pond's north end. Crows were more Daddy Joe's kind of guys anyway. He had known them all individually, in the Buck and Sis sense, and could have told you, from the tone of their yelling, whether these were feeling threatened or just cranky as usual.

There were signs that he hadn't been around in a while. His old boat was full of rainwater. The pond was rimmed with algal slime that he would have got rid of somehow. A black-gum over by his pine seedlings was stooped by a hanging pinoak limb that had blown off during one of the spring

storms. That honeysuckle, without his discipline, was pro-
liferating madly. He spent his last best years attending to such
matters, and he was genuinely happy doing it. The leisure of
retirement was no crisis for him; it was a delight. He had
enough clearing and burning, beaver cussing and teaching
children to crappie fish, to keep him busy for a century.

And Bruiser wondered, sitting there on the old picnic table
(which needed painting again), if it was really the disease that
had killed him, after all. Maybe it was the knowledge that he
wouldn't be able any more to get up early and come up the hill
and either neglect or attend to his "duties," depending on how
the catfish were biting.

His chronic happiness had baffled and even annoyed
Bruiser back when Bruiser was sappy with Voltaire and
ashamed that none of his kinfolks knew of Hegel. Daddy Joe
had spent his life doing the most demanding and unreward-
ing kinds of work and it seemed to young Bruiser that if
anyone had earned the right to be bitter or cynical or melancholy, his father had. Reared in the squalor of rural poverty,
Daddy Joe had been pulled out of the schoolhouse at fourteen
upon the death of his father, and put to work fulltime behind a
plow. He never had any education, any training, any luck at
making money. Soon after he and Polly married, as teenagers,
their first house, with everything in the world they called their
own inside it, burned to the ground.

While Bruiser was growing up, Daddy Joe worked nights,
three hundred sixty-five of them a year, as a watchman at the
Sheridan sawmill, keeping an hourly rendezvous with a series of time-clock punchkeys strung around a lumberyard,
and sometimes after supper Adolescent Bruiser would bum a
ride over to the mill and walk a round or two with him. It
always made the boy feel bad, and a bit embarrassed, that his
father had to give so much of his life to that endless uneventful
trudge. D.J. would be sitting on the tailgate of his pickup when
Bruiser got there, eating his chopped ham sandwich and
drinking coffee out of the lid of his Thermos and watching the
cars pass on the highway, going somewhere. The two of them
would soon start the slow trek over those dark, lonesome
trams, and even as a boy Bruiser would wonder:

Does he ever relieve the monotony by counting stars, or
making retirement plans, or trying to think of all the titles of
all the songs he's ever heard on the radio? Since he's never
been anywhere, does he wonder what all the places are like

that he might vaguely have heard tell of? Since he's not been exposed to books, save his Sunday School lesson book, does he speculate on what science might be about, or what it is that the hands of a wristwatch measure, or why some people are born with twelve toes? Has he ever projected himself into one of the airplanes passing overhead, or looked down at himself from Jupiter or the horn of Venus, or made love in his imagination to the gaunt sad goddess who gazes over his shoulder on the clear nights as he walks his solitary rounds? Does he count the number of steps he makes in a round and figure at the end if it's more or fewer than the average? Does he ever hit the average exactly? Does he ever calculate the number of rats, or bats, or luna moths, or stray dogs he sees on the average round? Does he ever think that if he has to make one more round he will go crazy and start screaming?

Not having been to college, Daddy Joe hadn't learned metaphysics, so he didn't dabble in such reflections as these. He was more of a Noah than a Job. One night there on the tram, Bruiser asked him: "When did you first come to work here?" and Daddy Joe said: "Aw, some time back yonder. I wadn't payin' no attention."

Bruiser had learned in college from J. Alfred Prufrock to abhor the thought of a man measuring out his life in coffee spoons, and, determined to get a statistical fix on his father's occupational burden, he carried the time-clock one night while they made the rounds together. He found that it took forty-seven minutes of the allotted hour to make the required circuit at a comfortable pace — through the drying sheds, the kilns, the boiler room, the sawing rooms, the control room, the business office, the loading dock. Forty-seven minutes each hour, eight hours each night, three hundred sixty five nights each year, for x number of years — walking a rut into the heavy old boards of that tram. That was the only statistic, the only answer to any of the questions, that Bruiser ever came up with. It was enough.

Daddy Joe didn't pay no attention to it, either, and only laughed softly at his son's curious interest in it. Hard as Bruiser tried, he just couldn't drag the old coot in under his little black cloud of proletarian outrage. Bruiser used all the coffee spoons he knew about — Marx's, Spengler's, Jefferson's, Orwell's, Franklin Roosevelt's, Tennessee Ernie Ford's — but Daddy Joe would just smile innocently at all the magnificent abstractions and would say, "You want a Co'-Cola, we'll stop by the boiler room and get one."

He simply wouldn't let himself be defined by his work. He knew there was more to his life than being a peon who owed his soul to the company store, and, like a Dickens urchin, the man had no complaints. He really didn't. So he had to paint houses six days a week, and trudge oxlike around a sawmill seven nights a week, just to preserve the distinction between poor and needy, with never the chance to learn, to travel, to articulate, to play rich folks just once, to win one piddling award that might season a bland obituary — well, so what? What he did got the young'uns fed and eventually reared them into people — a whole gang of people whom he loved and liked. And when he had worn the rut to the ordered depth, he could get on to the good work up there on the home place hill.

He had this to consider, too — and he did: he had a woman he was proud of and comfortable with, who never once in fifty-two years made him feel small. He had good neighbors, and was one. He was honest, decent, friendly and compassionate, and if there were those who took advantage of him because they didn't share those qualities, that was their problem, not his. And even before he built that pond, he found time to be monarch of just about every good fishing hole and patch of hunting woods in the bailiwick where he grew up, lived happily, forgot to notice that he was growing old, and died.

He considered himself a lucky man, despite all the crap he took from people who would have been surprised to know that they were his inferiors. And thinking himself a lucky man made him one, which was why you seldom saw him that he wasn't joking or kidding or laughing or smiling with somebody or chasing a child around the washpot. His last coherent words to Bruiser were just what they should have been. "Hey, Buck," he said weakly. "How's the boys?"

Bruiser laughed at that, and Daddy Joe managed a laugh, too, not knowing what the joke was, but not needing to.

Bruiser laughed about it again, sitting there on the picnic table at the pond.

And he recalled something that Sister Bet had said earlier in the day, there in the living room during the death watch: "I wonder," she said, "if he was ever depressed a single day in his whole life."

Bruiser knew, as he surveyed the brilliant springtime transformation of the environs that his father had loved, that the answer was no — depression like the dark angel had passed him over — and he had died in the grace of an innocence that itself wasn't long for this world.

CHAPTER SIXTEEN

Trick or Treat

Halloween was one of Bruiser's favorite holidays when he was growing up. The home place was far enough out in the country so that few city-slicker trick-or-treaters from Sheridan ventured out that way, and that meant less competition for the marvelous treats concocted for the occasion by the neighbor ladies — Mrs. West and Mrs. Land and Mrs. Anderton and them. They made candied apples, raisin cookies the size of Frisbees, popcorn balls big as your little brother's head, apricot fried pies with crusts so light and flaky that they threatened just to float away.

Losing out on that annual bonanza was one of Bruiser's genuine regrets about growing up. But he thought one of the real pleasures of parenthood would be introducing his own children to the Halloween tradition.

The time came at last when they were old enough to crawl into their ugly-old-witch and scary-skeleton costumes and go out trick-or-treating the first time. Their mother decreed that they were too young yet to go unchaperoned, and she gave Bruiser a choice: he could chauffer them around the neighborhood, or she would drive them while he stayed home and kept the candle lit in the jack-o-lantern and doled out the Tootsie Rolls to all the other goblins who would be out roaming the neighborhood and ringing the doorbell for handouts. Bruised opted for the driving job, partly out of nostalgia, partly because he wanted to make sure they experienced Halloween fully and properly, and partly because he thought it wouldn't take long. He could let Witch and Bones hit up a few of their

Pine Bluff neighbors for sweets, and they'd be back home in plenty of time for the kickoff of the television football game.

This plan went smoothly until Bruiser pulled the car up to the curb in front of the house of their first benefactor/victim.

"Now before you get out of the car," Bruiser told them, "let's go over this one more time. You go up the sidewalk, ring the doorbell, and when someone opens the door, you say 'Trick or treat!' and open your sack. Then you come back to the car and we drive to the next house. Simple, eh?"

"I get to ring the doorbell," said Scampette Witch.

"Why does *she* get to ring the doorbell?" said Bruiser Jr. Bones.

"I'm the oldest," Witch said.

"I can ring them good as you can."

"You can take *turns* ringing the doorbell," Bruiser said.

"I get to ring the first one," Witch said.

"Why does *she* get to ring the first one?" said Bones.

"Why don't you *both* put a finger on the button and push it at the same time?" Bruiser suggested diplomatically.

"What if they don't have a doorbell? Some houses don't have doorbells."

"Knock on the door, then."

"What if the people don't hear us knocking?"

"Knock real loud."

"Why does *she* get to knock? Why can't *I* knock?"

"You can both knock. Jeez, you two sure have a lot to learn about getting into the spirit of Halloween."

"What if a big dog jumps out and starts biting us?"

"These people don't have a dog."

"What if they've got a wolf?"

"They don't have a wolf, either."

"What if they've got a eagle with real sharp claws?"

"Hey, these are nice people. Mr. Chandler drives the Wonder Bread truck. You're not supposed to be scared of them; they're supposed to be scared of *you*."

But they continued to stall. Eventually they owned up to the reason: they wanted Bruiser to demonstrate for them how trick-or-treating was done. He agreed to go with them to the Chandlers' front door, just to get them past their first-mooch jitters. But they told him that wasn't what they meant. They wanted him to go to the door and get their candy while they waited in the safety of the car.

"No way," Bruiser told them. "Grown people don't trick-or-treat."

"Why not?"

"It's against the law. Besides, I don't have a costume."

"You can wear my mask," Bones said. "It's making me hot."

"You keep that mask on. And both of you get out of this car and go ring that doorbell or we're going home right now."

They made no move, so Bruiser put the car in gear and began to drive away. That started them crying. Over their wails, Bruiser lectured them on the importance of overcoming one's fears and marching right out into the world and boldly claiming one's share of the Milk Duds. He slowly circled the block while he lectured, easing to a stop again by the curb in front of the Chandler house.

They continued their piteous weeping until he broke down.

"All right, just this one house," he said. "Just to show you how easy it is."

And it *was* easy there. Mrs. Chandler donated two peppermint sticks — one for each sack — and Bruiser was a good sport about her witty greeting: "My, my, yours is the most frightening costume we've seen tonight."

The next house wasn't so easy, though. Witch and Bones refused to accompany him to that one, too, because there was no light on the front porch, and the hedge along the front walk looked like a perfect hiding place for Dracula. The people who rented this house had just moved in recently, and Bruiser wasn't acquainted with them. He thought he might take the opportunity to welcome them to the neighborhood while he was hitting them up for a couple of gumdrops or peanut patties.

A stout man with stubbly jowls answered the door. He reminded Bruiser of Bluto. He also resembled the burly cigar-chomping Disney wolf in the vintage-Forties cartoons. His beer belly sagged over his low-riding underwear boxer shorts, and he wore a grimy undershirt and thongs. He opened the door with a gruff, "Yeah, what is it?"

His appearance startled Bruiser, who began to stammer: "I'm, uh ... I mean, It's Halloween and all, and I'm, uh, well, I'm sort of trick-or-treating for my ..."

Bluto eyed him coldly and said: "Bums like you is the reason my taxes are so high."

Bruiser backed up a step and laughed nervously and said:

"No, you don't understand ... See, I'm not ... I mean, my kids are right out here in the car and ... well, what we're doing, we're, uh, tricking treaty, er, treating-tricky...trick, uh, ... we're collecting for UNICEF."

"Yuniwhat?"

"CEF ... You know, hungry children all over the world, and we're ..."

Bruiser backed off another step.

Bluto said: "You want a treat? How does a knuckle sandwich sound?"

Bruiser now began what the militarists call a tactical withdrawal. Backing away rather hurriedly, he caught the porch railing with his calf and did a perfect back flip into a prickly shrub by the front step.

It hadn't occurred to him before that the boy's fear of "eagles with real sharp claws" might have been a metaphor. He understood now, thanks to the several hundred talons of that holly bush. He managed to stifle most of his yeeches and yows as he scrambled to his feet, grabbed the two sacks on the run, and beat it back to the car.

"What happened?" Witch said.

"Did a big dog bite you and chase you?" Bones said.

"Heck no," Bruiser said, knowing that if he told them the truth they never *would* get out of the car. "I was just having some real trick-or-treat fun. Boy, this is *fun!* You guys don't know what you're missing."

Witch felt around in her sack and said, "Hey, wait a minute. You didn't get us any more candy at that house. All I got is this peppermint stick and now it's all broke."

Bruiser added another tangle to his web. "The nice man at that house didn't have any treats," he said. "But he gave me some money and said, 'Take those youngsters to the Dairy Queen and buy them a double-decker ice cream cone.' Wouldn't that be better than a sackful of gooey old candy?"

They agreed to the ice cream, but after eating it, they wanted Bruiser to take them trick-or-treating again. Or take *himself.* He refused.

"We made a deal," he said firmly. "Ice cream *instead* of more candy. Not ice cream *and* more candy."

They considered themselves to have been hoodwinked, and they bawled like coyotes as Bruiser drove them home. Witch was especially aggrieved. All her kindergarten friends would have great trick-or-treat stories for show-and-tell the next morning, she sobbed, but she would have to stand up there and admit shamefully that her mean old daddy gypped her out of the chance to participate in the funnest Halloween tradition.

Bones felt cheated, too.

"She got more ice cream than I did," he said between sobs. "Most of mine falled on the floor."

Sure enough, Bruiser looked around and saw the large chocolate puddle on the carpet of the back-seat floor.

He spoke various blasphemies and colloquialisms.

He stopped the car and tried to clean up the mess with the only cleaning materials he could find — the owner's manual and vehicle registration papers in the glove compartment.

Witch interrupted her crying long enough to attempt blackmail.

"If you'll take us tricky-treaten some more," she said, "we won't tell Momma you made us cry."

"No deal," Bruiser said, ladling up a gob of chocolate with the owner's manual and flinging it into the gutter beside the street.

"We won't tell her you said, 'Aw, son, bullshit.'"

"Nobody likes a dirty squealer," Bruiser said.

"He said 'son-of-a-bitch' too," Bones said.

Bruiser didn't really want to take them home right then. He would have to explain to Scamp how he had managed in a half-hour's time to turn what should have been a thrilling experience into one of tears and heartbreak, cursing and tattling, chocolate-smeared upholstery and two crumbled candy canes. He would have to explain that to *himself*. He didn't want Halloween poisoned for his family by bitter memories. And even if he had got home in time to watch that ball game, he wouldn't be able now to watch it in tranquillity.

So he let his children think they had successfully blackmailed him, which raised their little spirits considerably, although they *still* wouldn't get out of the car at the next house.

Bruiser was mistaken for a panhandler at that house, too, and told to scram. And at the next one, the lady of the house apparently sized him up as a would-be rapist and told him she would take pleasure in hacking off his arm with a butcher knife if he tried to reach in and tear the chain lock off her door.

At the rate he was going, he would be trick-or-treating at

Christmas, so Bruiser changed his strategy. A gang of juvenile "ghosts" happened to be working this street, and he borrowed Bones' skeleton mask and threw in with them. He cruised along behind them in the car, and when they made for a house, he hopped out and waddled up to the door behind them, walking in a painful hunker, ducklike. He shrouded himself with his trenchcoat, which was beige instead of white and which was something of a problem because it didn't have eyeholes, and tried to hang back in the crowd so that whoever answered the door wouldn't notice him. From his crouch, he thrust his two sacks in among the massed sheets and hoped that the candy-giver-outer assumed that the hairy forearms were just a clever costuming touch — Wolfman, maybe.

This ruse actually worked at two houses, and would have worked at the third, except that when the woman there was handing out the bite-size Butterfingers, a carload of teenagers wheeled around the corner and commenced to egg Bruiser's car. The chocolate floor was bad enough, but this would require a whole new automotive wash-and-wax, and Bruiser was concerned too about the safety of Witch and Bones. So, amidst all those ghosts who were half his height, he leapt to his feet and began to give the offenders chase, shouting epithets even coarser than those earlier ones. This alarmed the woman, whose husband responded to her yikes by unleashing their Great Dane, which began to give *Bruiser* chase. Sir Arthur Conan Doyle described this dog with uncanny accuracy in "The Hound of the Baskervilles." Bruiser did an acrobatic veer, and piled into his own car with not a second to spare, grateful to have lost only a lower pantsleg to the beast, and bearing only two minor wounds from fangs that were a good six inches apart and roughly the size of machetes.

While Bruiser hyperventilated, Bones said matter-of-factly: "I told you there was dogs."

Bruiser refused to go back home before redeeming the good name of Halloween for his children. He wanted them to know that there were still isolated pockets of neighborly generosity in this sorry old world; that vicious people were the exception; that bad dogs and Blutos were few and far between. It took another hour, but he collected enough confections to pacify the children and inspire the dentist to add on to his garage.

Witch and Bones wanted their mother to see in all its glory the treasure "they" had amassed, so they dumped it on the coffee table in the parlor. It was a disgusting compost heap of melted Reese cups, stale fig newtons and discolored jawbreakers, shaped into a sticky wad by marshmallows, nougat and caramel, and topped with crumbled cookie bits, stray pieces of candy corn, and tatters of foil from Hershey's kisses. It would have been right at home in the Metropolitan Museum of Modern Art. After shedding their costumes, Scampette and Bruiser Jr. devoured most of the pile before bedtime, ensuring a long night of colic and bad dreams.

Bruiser got to ponder that grotesque sculpture before they ate it, though, and he saw rising from it a familiar specter — Purple Rome, bloated from wretched excess, stumbling toward oblivion. It was only a fleeting vision of overindulgence, but it was sufficient to inspire the crusader in Bruiser. He decided then and there to found an international organization to abolish the secular celebration of All Saints Eve. (The acronym here turned out to be OATS CASE, not exactly one that burned itself into the mind, but never mind that.) The premise was that the Halloween duality had got all out of kilter: treats that didn't have razor blades in them would get the job done more slowly by arteriosclerosis; and insofar as tricks, nothing short of airplane hijackings even counted any more. If there weren't fried pies and popcorn balls to justify them, gluttony and vandalism didn't warrant their own holiday. Also, if OATS CASE accomplished nothing else, it could call for a moratorium on annual reruns of "It's the Great Pumpkin, Charlie Brown."

Bruiser used his considerable influence in the public prints to promote the campaign. He announced the results of a study showing that a person who trick-or-treated as a child was more likely to become a wino bumming quarters in his old age. He suggested an OSHA regulation to discourage interest in Halloween by requiring that all jack-o-lanterns be carved in such a way that they would bear a facial resemblance to the new president, Richard Nixon. He urged people to contact Halloween costume manufacturers and express the hope that they would be reincarnated as Tom Sawyer's cat.

None of this struck a chord, though, and so Halloween, with no stake through its heart, returned like remorse the following October. That year, Scampette, garbed as a ghost, cried because she wanted to be Pocahontas. Bruiser Jr., decked out in a pirate mask, cried because he wanted a wooden leg to go with it. Bruiser made them wear jackets because it was cold out, and Scampette cried because ghosts don't wear jackets. The rubber string holding the Long John Silver mask on Bruiser Jr.'s face broke, and he cried about that. Once they got out to the car, Bruiser discovered that vandals had soaped obscenities on the windshield, and *he* cried about that.

The only progress the following year was that the goblins agreed to accompany Bruiser when he rang doorbells and made his pitch. They stood flanking him with their sacks open. He considered amending his spiel to ask the donors to throw in a cookie for him, but the only profit he ever made was when Mr. Chandler offered him a pull from a flask while the missus doled out some fudge.

Bruiser was relieved when the young'uns finally got old enough to fiend for themselves. He stepped down as executive secretary and sole member of OATS CASE, and left the fate of a gluttonous society in other hands. He penned his letter of resignation on the Halloween night when a chartered busload of trick-or-treaters arrived in his neighborhood at two a.m., many of them carrying designer sacks, and a couple smoking cigars.

ttle Pine Bluff subdivision. A good name for this subdivision
ould have been Modesto, but it was called Broadmoor. The
ame was a mystery because Broadmoor wasn't broad and it
ad no moors like Wuthering Heights nor any Moors like
thello. Many of the suburban housing developments of
ruiser's America, if not most of them, bore similarly myster-
us names. Bruiser in time would live near a Crestview with
o crest to view, a Quail Ridge with no quail and no ridge, and
Maple Creek Farms that was as much of a triptych mis-
omer as the Holy Roman Empire. But he wasn't as inclined
some of his more urbane acquaintances to regard these
nony names as symptomatic of a phony, sterile, shallow
iburban way of life. Even before suburban housing develop-
ents, most men lived lives of quiet desperation; and Bruiser
;sumed that developers chose names like Broadmoor and
restview instead of more accurate names like Tacky Flats
id Cookie Cutter Fringe from the same muddled impulse
iat inspired people to put plastic flowers on what might
herwise be dignified and perfectly attractive graves.

Broadmoor offered the bourgeois life that Bruiser had as-
red to, but once he had settled into it he had most of the
nventional complaints. He was amazed that the people of
iiwan made so many unassembled things that the suburban
merican family didn't think it could do without. Here's one
iat somebody gave Bruiser and Scamp as an expensive house-
arming gift: a trash compactor. They were still lacking most
f the practical appliances, furnishings and decorations, but
iey would always hereafter be able to compact their trash.

One of Suburban Bruiser's first tasks was to put up a made-
-Taiwan television antenna. This was a chore that Daddy
ie would have completed in about five minutes because D.J.
dn't care how a thing looked if he could get it to work; but
ruiser had to take into account several not-so-practical sub-
-ban considerations. He had to put the antenna on the back
le of the house, for instance, because it was ugly and he
dn't want people driving by the suburban dream home
ying, "Well, that might be a decent-looking little hovel
:cept for that eyesore television antenna." Putting the an-
nna on the back of the house complicated the task con-
derably because the television receiver had to go in a room at
e *front* of the house. That meant Bruiser had to run the antenna
ire from the top of the antenna, through an attic vent at the
ick of the house, through the attic, out another attic vent at

CHAPTER SEVENTEEN

Attic Shape

Munchkin Manor was too small for a fami[ly]
when his weekly salary skyrocketed to the thresh[old]
figures, Bruiser found time between hoorawi[ng]
welcoming spring to move his brood to a larger a[nd]
better part of the city.

The new place was a brick duplex, with [the]
landlady living on the other side. Scamp called [it]
That wasn't altogether because it had the look [of a]
dungeon. It was also because the landlady, Mrs[.]
look and manner about her that suggested a pris[on]

Mrs. Cobb looked as rough as her name. She w[as]
square-jawed, had a deep voice and rolled her [own]
from a pull-string sack of Bull Durham. She wa[s]
ly, but Bruiser was scared of her. He suspected th[at she]
would grab him by the elbow, sling him up over [her]
smash him down on the top of a parked car, just [to]
it.

Sing Sing was just a stopover in the Bruise[r]
suburbs. Bruiser had a notion that he would n[ever]
who he was as long as he remained a squatter [in someone]
else's digs. He and Scamp wanted to live in a re[al home]
that the finance company would good-naturedl[y call]
their own. In Pine Bluff, as in most American cit[ies]
— a time when the inner cities had died and [a new]
approach to rehabilitating them had been found [in]
the suburbs. They soon found just what they we[re after]
— a modest little house with a modest little yar[d]

the front of the house, down the outside front wall, through a window, down the inside wall, under the rug, across the floor to the opposite inside wall, and eighteen inches up that wall to connect there with the television set.

The trickiest part of this antenna-wire odyssey would be the crossing of the attic. There was less than four feet of crawlspace in this attic and Bruiser was more than six feet tall. That meant he would have to pull the unattached end of the antenna wire from the rear attic vent to the front attic vent in a balled-up crouch or a bear-like crawl, and he would have to make this contorted forty-foot trek on a path only two inches wide, scooting along one of the ceiling rafters; if he ventured or slipped off that rafter, the only thing between him and rubble-strewn death on the living room floor far below would be a few fibers of insulation and a flimsy half-inch of ceiling drywall.

Getting a television antenna wire across an attic seemed to Bruiser an ignoble cause to risk his life for. But suburban American people risked their lives for such causes all the time. They got up on long unsteady ladders to clean dead leaves out of their gutters. They fiddled with live wires when they were installing clothes driers. They struck matches looking for gas leaks around hot-water heaters. And if they got their eyebrows burnt off occasionally, or slipped a disc or two, or lost a minor appendage, well, that was a small price to pay for the good life. Bruiser learned to perform such daredeviltry without even thinking of the danger.

Before he could get that antenna wire through his attic, he first had to get *into* the attic. The only entrance was through a small bedroom closet that had a removable ceiling panel at the top. Bruiser wedged a stool into the closet, hopped up on the stool, removed the panel and poked his head into the attic. It was the first time anyone had viewed this place since Dante Alligheri toured it with the shade of the Roman poet Vergil more than six hundred years before. The crawlspace was as dark as the inside of Jay Gould's heart, and despite the tiny front and back vents, it was as airless as a mummy's lung, as smothery as the breath of a cigar-smoker lover. Since this was a mid-August midafternoon, it was also hotter than blazes.

The closet-top opening was so small that Bruiser thought he might have to Vaseline his torso to get through, but with some hard twisting and squirming, he got his head and shoulders through the hole. His hands were still below, though, pinned painfully tight against his hips, and his flashlight was in one of them. The only way he could get the flashlight up was by reversing the alimentary process, so he decided to go back down. Drop back to the stool, toss up the flashlight, and make a more streamlined entrance, hands-first. But he discovered that he couldn't *get* back down. He wiggled and heaved and hula-ed, but couldn't budge. He was stuck fast, caught in a pose that parodied the great human dualities, dangling between Heaven and Hell, between the darkness and the light.

"Hey! This really *is* like being buried alive!" the right half of his brain shouted. "Somebody get me out of here quick! Help! Help!"

Bruiser yelled to Scamp, who was waiting below, but she couldn't hear him because his midriff tallow had the opening to the attic hermetically sealed. His increasingly frantic kicking and jerking convinced her after a time that he was stuck, and she removed the stool, grabbed his knees and pulled with all her might.

"Death! Tomb! Horror! Help! Help!"

Scamp finally got him down, and it took the steadying of several pulls at a flask to get him ready to try again. He got through the hole without incident on the second try. From his painful coalminer-style crouch, he shined the flashlight around to get his bearings and mark his route. He couldn't see much because the flashlight beam was scattered by the biggest collection of spider webs since the fall of the House of Usher. That inspired two of Freud's famous patients, Little Hans and the Russian Wolfman, to add to the panic.

"Mein Gott!" exclaimed Hans. "All black widows!"

"Nyet, ta*ran*tulas!" the Wolfman cried.

"Tarantulas!" wailed Hemi Right. "Oh, Lord! And we couldn't make a quick exit even if a whole swarm of them jumped on us. Look! There's one over your head right now, about to drop down your neck!"

Bruiser tried to look up but the crawlspace was so shallow that he succeeded only in scraping his forehead and nose on the underside of the roof.

"Come on, you guys, give me a break," he said.

His eyes gradually adjusted to the dark, and he saw the tiny vent at the rear of the attic, with the unattached end of the antenna wire poked through it. To get there, he could leapfrog perpendicularly across the ceiling rafters — or *creep*frog across them — but Hemi Right made him put his head back through little Pine Bluff subdivision. A good name for this subdivision would have been Modesto, but it was called Broadmoor. The name was a mystery because Broadmoor wasn't broad and it had no moors like Wuthering Heights nor any Moors like Othello. Many of the suburban housing developments of Bruiser's America, if not most of them, bore similarly mysterious names. Bruiser in time would live near a Crestview with no crest to view, a Quail Ridge with no quail and no ridge, and a Maple Creek Farms that was as much of a triptych misnomer as the Holy Roman Empire. But he wasn't as inclined as some of his more urbane acquaintances to regard these phony names as symptomatic of a phony, sterile, shallow suburban way of life. Even before suburban housing developments, most men lived lives of quiet desperation; and Bruiser assumed that developers chose names like Broadmoor and Crestview instead of more accurate names like Tacky Flats and Cookie Cutter Fringe from the same muddled impulse that inspired people to put plastic flowers on what might otherwise be dignified and perfectly attractive graves.

Broadmoor offered the bourgeois life that Bruiser had aspired to, but once he had settled into it he had most of the conventional complaints. He was amazed that the people of Taiwan made so many unassembled things that the suburban American family didn't think it could do without. Here's one that somebody gave Bruiser and Scamp as an expensive housewarming gift: a trash compactor. They were still lacking most of the practical appliances, furnishings and decorations, but they would always hereafter be able to compact their trash.

One of Suburban Bruiser's first tasks was to put up a made-in-Taiwan television antenna. This was a chore that Daddy Joe would have completed in about five minutes because D.J. didn't care how a thing looked if he could get it to work; but Bruiser had to take into account several not-so-practical suburban considerations. He had to put the antenna on the back side of the house, for instance, because it was ugly and he didn't want people driving by the suburban dream home saying, "Well, that might be a decent-looking little hovel except for that eyesore television antenna." Putting the antenna on the back of the house complicated the task considerably because the television receiver had to go in a room at the *front* of the house. That meant Bruiser had to run the antenna wire from the top of the antenna, through an attic vent at the back of the house, through the attic, out another attic vent at

CHAPTER SEVENTEEN

Attic Shape

Munchkin Manor was too small for a family of four. So when his weekly salary skyrocketed to the threshhold of three figures, Bruiser found time between hoorawing Mao and welcoming spring to move his brood to a larger apartment in a better part of the city.

The new place was a brick duplex, with the widowed landlady living on the other side. Scamp called it Sing Sing. That wasn't altogether because it had the look and feel of a dungeon. It was also because the landlady, Mrs. Cobb, had a look and manner about her that suggested a prison warden.

Mrs. Cobb looked as rough as her name. She was blocky and square-jawed, had a deep voice and rolled her own smokes from a pull-string sack of Bull Durham. She wasn't unfriendly, but Bruiser was scared of her. He suspected that one day she would grab him by the elbow, sling him up over her head, and smash him down on the top of a parked car, just for the hell of it.

Sing Sing was just a stopover in the Bruiser flight to the suburbs. Bruiser had a notion that he would never find out who he was as long as he remained a squatter in somebody else's digs. He and Scamp wanted to live in a real house, one that the finance company would good-naturedly let them call their own. In Pine Bluff, as in most American cities at the time — a time when the inner cities had died and no effective approach to rehabilitating them had been found — that meant the suburbs. They soon found just what they were looking for — a modest little house with a modest little yard in a modest the hole and take some deep breaths before starting out. In the heat, he was sweating like a prizefighter, and thoughtful Scamp, standing below, swabbed his face with a cloth, which she had tied to the end of a broomstick.

He reached the rear vent without calamity. That was the easy part. Now he had to take the antenna wire and inch his way laterally along a single rafter to the front vent. The safest way would be to get down on all-fours and crawl bearlike along the rafter. Or he could put his toes on one rafter and his hands on the next parallel rafter over and sidle sideways like a crab toward the front vent. But either way would require the full use of his hands. And he needed at least one hand free to hold the flashlight and the end of the antenna wire. He could carry the antenna wire between his teeth, but there was still the flashlight. He could leave the flashlight on one of the rafters, with its lightbeam pointing to his destination, but Hemi Right, Little Hans, and the Wolfman unanimously vetoed that idea quicker than a meaningful Security Council resolution.

No, he would have to make the crossing with the light in one hand and the wire in the other, negotiating the rafter in the manner of a tightrope walker — a hunchbacked, balled-up, claustrophobic, zoophobic, semi-hysterical tightrope walker.

Before he embarked, Hemi Right insisted that he stick his nose through the slatting of the rear attic vent and take a few more breaths. The vent slatting was horizontal, like a partially closed venetian blind, and to get his nose out, Bruiser had to twist his head to an angle that was an anatomical impossibility. His topmost vertebra snapped ominously, and at the same instant he saw the wasp nest at the opposite corner of the vent, not eight inches in front of his wedged-between-the-slats proboscis. The nest had about a dozen large wasps crawling around on it.

Little Hans fainted on the spot. The Wolfman took out a gun and shot himself. Hemi Right went absolutely crazy and tried to sprout emergency wings and actually fly back to the closet-top escape hatch. Bruiser managed to avert disaster only because he had twisted his neck into such a grotesque position that he was temporarily paralyzed.

His presence agitated the wasps, but not quite to the point of attack, and as he stood there paralyzed, with his nose out the vent, they seemed to settle down a bit. Bruiser knew what he should do next. He should ease slowly, ever so slowly, away from the danger, along his rafter toward the front vent, taking care to keep the antenna wire coming through the side of the vent away from the wasp nest. But knowing what action he should take is no great advantage to a man who is paralyzed. Bruiser couldn't move. And he couldn't call Scamp to come help because his proximity to the wasps made it probable that even a whisper would put them on maneuvers.

If the gods had been directing this farce, they would have left him there forever — twisted like a pretzel, terrified, boiling in his own sweat, with his nose sticking out an attic vent. The gods petrify people in positions like that sometimes to remind succeeding generations that men aren't gods. But Bruiser didn't sense that his attic shape was a candidate for the stony immortality of Niobe or Aglauros. His situation was too silly for posterity to take any useful instruction from it. And yet here was an example of the kinship between a low form of comedy and a high type of torment, and Bruiser wondered if it didn't deserve some sort of memorialization, if not on a Grecian urn, then maybe on two billion plastic, large-size, free-with-the-purchase-of-a-Burger King Whopper soft-drink cups.

He subsequently wrote a letter to Norman Rockwell describing the scene with his nose out the attic vent. "Only one of your inimitable paintings could do it justice," the letter said. "Only you could capture the poignancy and pathos and challenge of suburban life in modern America that is revealed here."

Norman Rockwell never answered this letter, and Bruiser, upon reflection, was glad. Because the scene was worthy of a greater artist than Rockwell; it was worthy of Picasso.

In his letter to Picasso, Bruiser wrote: "I know it would be compositionally awkward to show both me in the attic darkness and my nose outside in the August sunlight. So how about this? — how about if you just paint the outside wall with a nose sticking out of the attic vent. It's not important to show who the nose belongs to, or even the wasps. What do you say?"

Picasso never said anything, and Bruiser finally took the idea to Anton Smith, the Arkansas artist. Here is what Anton Smith said: "Yeah, well, let me get back to you on that."

The consensus of artistic indifference made Bruiser wonder. Maybe there wasn't as much existential significance as he had supposed in that nose sticking out that vent. Maybe he was hoping to immortalize the nose just because it was his. Maybe the lingering questions weren't even worth asking: (1) Did he overcome his paralysis and get away without getting stung? (2) Or did the dust on the slats of the vent cause him to sneeze, rousing the wasps and causing him to flee wildly and go crashing through the living room ceiling? (3) Did he get to the other side of the attic Wallenda style, or Gentle Ben style, or Cancer the Crab style? (4) Did he get to the other side at all? (5) Did he get the wire hooked up and sit back to enjoy the rewards of his toil only to have the goddam picture tube blow out?

The gods would have left those questions unanswered, and the painters would have, and the slice-of-life story writers would have, and Mrs. Cobb wouldn't have been able to resist getting a long fishing pole and jabbing the wasp nest. But this is one of those rare tales in which the mischievous do not finally have their way; it is a tale of brief Broadmoor triumph, and the answers are yes, no, Wallenda style, yes, and yes.

CHAPTER EIGHTEEN

Flight

The flight to the suburbs was the beginning of an odyssey that would lead Bruiser to other cities, other states, other lands, before he completed the circle back to his own Ithica. It was one of the beliefs of his time that moving around was the way to move up — and not only in an occupational sense. The running man was a popular theme in books like *Rabbit, Run* and movies like *Five Easy Pieces* and songs like *By the Time I Get to Phoenix*. The suggestion here was that to stay put was to stultify, and the implication was that in order to find himself a person needed to run away from wherever he was and look somewhere else; that self-realization came through movement, action, change of scene. Bruiser accepted all of that pretty passively, although not to the point of abandoning his family and chasing off after some cult or altered state or illusion of freedom. His flight was one of short hops, with awkward landings, like that of the gooney bird.

His first landing was in Little Rock, the capital of Arkansas, where he was newspaper commentator on rassling and other Proustian topics for the *Arkansas Democrat*. He thought he would like the change from Pine Bluff's miasmal flats to the green hills of Little Rock, and he did mostly, but one thing nobody told him was that those hills were alive with tarantulas. These weren't the imaginary tarantulas of the Russian wolfman; these were the real McCoy — black and hairy and horrible — and it was just Bruiser's luck to arrive in Little Rock at the height of the annual tarantula trek to higher ground.

He was still unpacking the U-Haul when he heard some of the neighborhood youngsters — a group of them hanging out on their bikes down by the curb — talking about maybe capturing a whole slew of tarantulas and staging some kind of giant tarantula war. This was neat, hanging-out, creepy-movie-type kid talk, he thought, an updated version of the cops-and-robbers and cowboys-and-Indians fantasies that had occupied him as a youngster back at the home place. As best he could recall from his high-school biology textbook, the nearest real-life tarantulas were in Brazil. Or maybe the desert out west. He had lived his entire life within an hour's drive of the Arkansas hills and never, ever, had he heard that they might harbor such monsters. But while he was pondering the tarantula geography, one of those urchins there by the curb pulled something out of a jar and offered to let him pet it. Gadzooks, it looked like Charlie Chaplain's hat! Bruiser jumped straight up in the air, and ran into the house hyperventilating.

A while later, Mrs. Purvis, his new next-door neighbor, dropped over, and when Bruiser mentioned tarantulas, she laughed and said yes, she'd had to kick two or three of the little scudders out of the way in the yard just now. "I know they're harmless," she said, "but sometimes they sure do get in the way."

Bruiser's response to that was: "Harmless? Is a heart attack harmless? That's what I'll have the first time one crawls into bed with me. Is a car wreck harmless? That's what I'll have the first time I'm driving to work and one jumps up on my shoulder from the back seat."

The next morning, as Bruiser headed out to the garage, late for work, he found three of them blocking the path to the door of his car. They looked like eight-legged bowling balls. He would have preferred to scatter them with a bazooka or some hand grenades, but had to make do with a broom handle, which he used like a lance to try to prod or nudge the first one out of his way. Instead of scampering off, it reared on its hind legs and proposed to duke it out. It snapped its jaws menacingly, and when Bruiser persisted, it snatched the broomstick out of his grasp and threw it across the driveway into the shrubs.

Bruiser scurried back into the house.

"Forget something?" Scamp said.

"We're moving."

"We just *got* here."

"I don't care. I can live with the threat of nuclear holocaust; I can live where there's crime and rats and big old vicious dogs running loose and vampire bats swooping down out of the air, but I can't live in a neighborhood where a gang of hood tarantulas come around demanding protection money."

"It's their migration season, I read in the paper. It says there's really not very many of them and they'll be gone in a few days."

"No, in a few days *I'll* be gone."

But she shamed him into going back out to face them. "You won't ever conquer these irrational fears till you confront them," she said.

"It's not fears I'm worried about confronting right now," he said. "Listen, these things could get jobs as bellhops."

The tarantulas hadn't moved, and there was no way around them, so Bruiser dragged his daughter's bicycle out of the storage room, took it down to the end of the driveway, pedaled it furiously to get up some speed, put his feet up on the handlebars lest a tarantula leap up and bite off one of his legs, and coasted toward the car, swerving three times to try to smash the invader beasts with the bicycle tires.

He smashed instead into the side of the garage.

That caused a shelf to collapse and a large collection of old cans and glassware and stuff to come raining down on him.

But in spite of the broken glass, the driveway oil slick, the polyester frays, and the raspberry on his knee, Bruiser considered this attack a success because all the racket and commotion caused the tarantulas to move away to what they presumably considered a safe distance. Bruiser took advantage of their momentary uncertainty and made a dash for the car door. Maybe they tried to cut him off, trip him up, throw him down, and swarm him like piranhas — or maybe not. Once in the car, he didn't have to think about them again.

Not until he was heading home from work that afternoon, and he turned into the driveway, and there they were, waiting for him. Not just the original three, who, it turned out, were just runts as tarantulas go, or maybe tarantula *children*. They had called up reinforcements, and these guys were *really* big.

CHAPTER NINETEEN

The Paramecium Complex

The laffs columnist for the *Arkansas Democrat* served as something of a community ambassador for the newspaper. So Bruiser not only wrote pithy anecdotes and rassling reports, he also judged spelling bees and poster contests; he was the designated back-seat waver in the official *Democrat* parade car, and he once served as celebrity finger on the local Dialing for Dollars television program. Bruiser didn't mind these duties as a rule, but one ambassadorial task that he didn't like was judging pet shows.

There were no good losers at pet shows, and some of the poorer losers had given Bruiser the Pet Show Judge a hard time of it. One had set a runner-up cocker spaniel on him; Billy the Boa Constrictor's losing owner had warned him that Billy would be paying him a revenge visit in the middle of the night; he had been sworn at in Portuguese by a losing macaw. Half a dozen of these unhappy aftermaths convinced him to forswear pet-show judging, and he was cajoled into an encore only by a truly moving and eloquent appeal from a grammar school principal who'd forgot until the last minute to line up some judges for his school's annual Pets on Parade.

Bruiser dreaded the thing but the appointed day turned out to be a beautiful one and he arrived at the schoolyard in what could then still be called a gay disposition. The youngsters had assembled quite a menagerie — dogs and cats of every description, parakeets and canaries and a mynah bird duo named Cisco and Pancho, box turtles and grass snakes and white rabbits and white mice, hamsters and squirrels, a lamb and a gander, goldfish and guppies, frogs and tadpoles, an organ-grinder's monkey and a rhinosceros beetle. This was before the pet rock craze, so there were no rocks, but one rich boy, having been turned down on his request to truck in his string of polo ponies, showed up with a giant Doberman that ate several other contestants before the day was done. Bruiser had always got on well with animals and the din of woofing, yapping, hissing, tweeting, croaking, chattering, honking, bleating and squawking made him feel good. He had a nice chat with Cisco and Pancho about Gertrude Stein's "Pigeons In The Grass, Alas," and it didn't even completely exorcise his high spirits when the grasshopper he maimed by thumping it off his shirtsleeve was revealed to be a contestant in the show and the pride and joy of a handicapped little orphan girl named Denise.

There were four other judges and they were arguing when Bruiser entered the judging room. Their dispute concerned the eligibility of a would-be contestant named Fred. Fred was an amoeba, or paramecium. Two of the judges wanted to let him participate in the show, and two were opposed. The two anti-Fred judges were a retired Air Force colonel and a certified public accountant. They argued that a pet, in order to qualify as a pet, should be visible to the naked eye. They also said a pet should be somehow lovable, should not be transparent, and should have readily recognizable features that could be compared to the features of the other entries and judged appropriately. Legs, for instance. The two judges who wanted to accept Fred were a lawyer and a housewife. The lawyer insisted that it would be unconstitutional to discriminate against unicellular micro-organisms, and the housewife didn't want it said that mean old judges sent Fred's owner home crying.

Bruiser's was the swing vote and he cast it in favor of Fred.

"Okay," the colonel said, "but I'm here to tell you I don't appreciate it one bit."

"Oh, come on, Harry, it's not World War Three," said the CPA, who was trying to be a good sport. "These are just kids."

"Well, how would you feel, Pete," the colonel said, "if you had a nice dog and had to go home and tell your folks it got beat out by a speck of slimy goo?"

"Just because we let him enter," said Pete the CPA, "doesn't mean we have to let him win."

"What did Fred ever do to *you?*" Bruiser said to the colonel.

"I just don't like ... germs," the colonel said. "I don't like you, either, Budzo. You look like the kind, if war came, who'd give up without a fight."

Bruiser's hackles went up. "Look, Pops," he said, "I don't know what your problem is, but — "

At this point the CPA and the housewife interceded, preventing a rumble, and Fred was duly entered into the competition, wriggling on a glass slide — his presence verified by the microscope that his third-grade owner had thoughtfully brought along.

This was a democratic pet show in that every pet was automatically entered in every category, so the judges were obliged to consider Fred along with all the other competitors for Happiest Pet, Most Unusual Pet, Most Beautiful Pet, Best Groomed Pet, Pet with the Longest (and Shortest) Tail, Pet with the Biggest (and Smallest) Ears, and so on. There were a dozen categories in all.

Bruiser nominated Fred for Most Unusual Pet, and the lawyer seconded the nomination.

"Now hold on," the colonel said. "I thought we had an agreement that this goo-ball wouldn't win anything."

"We said he didn't *have* to win," the lawyer said. "We didn't say he *couldn't.*"

"Now you're giving me a bunch of left-wing lawyer double-talk," the colonel said.

"Which one do *you* think's most unusual, Harry?" the CPA said.

"I think we ought to give it to a real pet," the colonel said. "One with a little bit of personality."

"That's a pathetic fallacy," Bruiser said.

"Pathetic is right, Budzo," the colonel said. "What do we do if he splits in two before the show's over? Answer me that. Which one of him do we give the prize to?"

"Him?" the housewife said. "If he splits, one would be a him and the other a her, isn't that the way it works? We'd have a Fred and a Freda."

A general science teacher happened to be in attendance, working in the concession stand outside, and his opinion was solicited. He wasn't sure but imagined that sexual differentiations were lost on parameciums.

"There you go," the colonel said. "We not only got ourselves a blob, we got a damn transvestite blob. I hope you people understand what you're doing, exposing our youngsters to this filth. I nominate the tadpole for most unusual."

"The tadpole!" Bruiser said.

"Yeah, the tadpole. You want to make something of it?"

"Talk about your goo-ball! Talk about no personality!"

"At least you can *see* a tadpole, Budzo. It don't sneak around invisible, commiting all these perverted sex acts."

"I second the motion on the tadpole," said Pete the CPA. "I don't know why but I do."

The lawyer called for a vote and it was three to two. Against the tadpole. For Fred.

"I'm afraid we've got a problem here," Pete the CPA said. "Smallest Ears and Shortest Tail will have to go to the paramecium, too, won't they? I mean, is there any logical way around that?"

"How do we know he's even *got* ears and a tail?" the colonel said. "Look through here and tell me if you see a tail or some ears on this thing."

The judges took turns gawking at Fred through the microscope.

"I don't see any ears or tail," the lawyer testified.

"There's something sticking out the top that might be a tail," Bruiser said.

"Let me look," the colonel said angrily.

He looked, then said, "Ha! That's no tail."

"How do you know it's not?" Bruiser said testily.

"It's sure wagging like a tail," said Pete the CPA.

"I don't see anything," the housewife said when it came her turn to gawk.

"What'd I tell you?" the colonel gloated. "No tail."

"I mean I don't see anything at *all*."

"What!" the colonel said, crowding her away from the microscope. "Let me see."

"My God!" he said then. "The pervert's escaped."

Fred's owner was summoned. After a few moments of high suspense, he maneuvered the slide around and relocated Fred, whose tail was still wagging happily.

"Definitely not a tail," the colonel said. "It's just a hair, or an antenna, like an ant or butterfly has."

"Even if it's not his tail," Bruiser said, "that doesn't prove anything. Maybe his tail is so prize-deservingly short, and his ears so prize-deservingly small, that this microscope can't pick them up."

"It's people with attitudes like that," the colonel said, "who've got the world in the shape it's in."

The lawyer called the science teacher back to the witness stand. The science teacher testified that in his opinion it wouldn't be unjust to deny Fred the short-tail and small-ears awards. Even if parameciums have ears and tails, he said, "they perhaps do not suit the traditional pet-show definitions of those anatomical phenomena."

"Exactly what I've been telling these nitwits," the colonel said.

"Listen, Pops, I won't sit here and be insulted by an old blowhard like you," Bruiser said.

"Yeah, Harry," said Pete the CPA, "this is supposed to be a fun event and you're being a real jerk."

"Jerk?" the colonel said.

"I think blowhard is more like it," Bruiser said.

"I think you owe us all an apology, Harry," Pete the CPA said. "Especially Mrs. Hollingshead."

"I didn't mean anything personal," the colonel said dryly. "Sorry if I offended anybody. Since we eliminated the goo-ball, I nominate the tadpole for the short tail award."

"What about the tarantulas?" Mrs. Hollingshead said.

"What about 'em? Spiders don't have tails."

"Proportionally speaking," the lawyer interjected, "the tadpole's tail is actually quite long."

"Well the tadpole *sure* ought to get the smallest ears," the colonel said. "Screw him out of that one and I say this whole contest is rigged."

"If I thought you meant that, Harry," said Pete the CPA, "I'd be the first to punch you in the nose."

"Does a tadpole even *have* ears?" said Mrs. Hollingshead.

"He does if a tarantula has a tail, sister. You tell me, does a tarantula have a tail? I'm sure not going to get down real close and *see* if he does, are you?"

"You don't have to be so hostile about everything, do you?" Mrs. Hollingshead said.

"I just resent being party to a scam," the colonel said.

"You're cruisin' for a bruisin', Pops," Bruiser said.

"You sure are intent on giving the tadpole a prize," the lawyer said to the colonel. "Any special reason?"

"Are you accusing me of something, Shylock?"

"You're the one brought up the subject of unfair judging,

Harry," said Pete the CPA.

"Yeah, Pops, 'fess up," Bruiser said.

"You people are a disgrace," the colonel said. "So what if the boy with the tadpole delivers my newspaper. He does a real good job. Up at five a.m., getting rained on, freezing to death. What am I supposed to tell him? — 'Sorry, Dwayne, your tadpole was a flop.'"

The judges decided diplomatically to consult with the science teacher again about tadpole ears, but the teacher had absconded, probably having anticipated such an imbroglio.

A compromise candidate, the rhinosceros beetle, got the small ears award.

The colonel nominated the tadpole for happiest pet, but Bruiser countered with a nomination for the goldfish, which, he said, though outwardly expressionless, seemed to have about it an aura of contentedness that indicated a clear conscience and an inclination to gladheartedness.

"That's the biggest crock I've ever heard," the colonel said. "I know happiness when I see it, and I'm telling you that tadpole is one happy little son-of-a-bitch."

"Just calm down, Harry," said Pete the CPA. "We'll think of some award to give the tadpole. We'll make one up if we have to. We don't want the boy to start throwing your paper on the roof."

"Well, we can't name him most beautiful," the colonel said. "He's got a lot going for him but not good looks. Even for a tadpole, he's no Rudolf Valentino."

"I nominate the Irish setter for most beautiful," said Mrs. Hollingshead. "We ought to give one award to a plain old cat or dog, don't you think?"

The haggling went on and on. By four-to-one votes, Cisco and Pancho shared the Pet of the Year award and a grass snake with a bow around its neck copped Best Groomed Pet. Honor was bestowed upon a cat. Posthumous certificates of merit memorialized various rodent and amphibian contestants eaten by the Doberman. Bruiser gradually lost track of the proceeding, voting rather mindlessly with the majority while he sank into a reverie.

He couldn't get Fred Paramecium out of his thoughts. Within a short time, Fred would have become Fred/Freda, then Fred/Freda/Freddy/Fredette, then an octet, splitting and re-splitting, a gathering, a throng, the original Fred lost in a googol of parameciums, every one of them Fred and yet none of them Fred. Would there still be a *real* Fred — what the Germans might call a *Ur-*Fred — a Fred with a legitimate claim to that Most Unusual Pet award?

Bruiser daydreamed that he was gawking at Fred through the microscope when Fred shaped his protoplasm into the likeness of a human face. The infinitesimal face was Bruiser's own, looking back at him. It looked back at him placidly, serenely, with a mild curiosity. Then it began to contort. It became enlongated, mashed, stretched, then it snapped in two, and two tiny Bruiser faces looked out at Bruiser. And soon four. Anon Bruiser was as piecemeal as Old Germany, as scattered as the stars. He was numberless, and as he watched himself continue to proliferate, the sensation was a magnification of what he had felt as he watched that alien version of himself chased by Murtha and the bear.

Were all of these Bruisers imposters, mockeries, caricatures?

He had assumed that his identity and his fate would clarify as he got older. But he wondered now if that wasn't just a pathetic fallacy of a different kind.

CHAPTER TWENTY

Pilgrimage

The religious quest was fashionable for a time there, when pilgrims from old critics like Malcolm Muggeridge to old rapists like Eldridge Cleaver were claiming to have found in Jesus the strength and inspiration to cope with their own existential misgivings, and Bruiser found their testimony tempting. They were more persuasive, he thought, than satanists or Maoists or acid-heads. So while the Beatles were making a similar pilgrimage to their guru in the Himalayas, Bruiser drove from Little Rock back to Sheridan one weekend to pay a call on the greatest religious authority he knew, his Great-aunt Laura Bell Stuckey.

He reviewed the varieties of his religious experience as he drove along, and the hour's drive took him back more years than miles — back to what his children, intending no derision, called the Good Old Days: back beyond the trauma of Little League, beyond even the tinkertoy time when all he wanted for Christmas was his two front teefe.

He was born on a Saturday and attended his first church service eight days later. He remembered that service well, if only because it was indistinguishable from all the others he would attend during the next eighteen years. On just about any Sunday morning between the Roosevelt twilight and the Kennedy dawn, you could have found him in the spartan nave of the First Christian Church in Sheridan, loving God and singing the praises of Gladly the Crosseyed Bear. Bruiser's family on both sides were stalwarts in this little Campbellite church; his mother and father had met in it as youngsters when the world itself was young in the Wilson ascendancy. Daddy Joe gave his blushing future bride a bold wink from the choirloft the first time he ever saw her.

Little Bruiser started out in their faithful footsteps. He was baptized when he was ten, along with the ringwormy Davis brothers. Getting baptized in Sheridan was like getting vaccinated against smallpox: it was something that everybody did once, when they were too young to understand it, so they never had to think about it again. The immersion was said to assure Little Bruiser of at least a bleachers seat in Heaven by washing away all the sins he had committed during those wicked years when he was learning to walk, to pee in the toilet, and to avoid eating dirt and toejam. (He always knew the Lord hated toejam eaters but the Devil is just irresistible sometimes.) This "blessed assurance," as the hymn called it, meant less to Bruiser than to his mother, who honestly exulted that all her brood, dutifully dunked and thus immortalized, would be with her in the sweet by and by. It pleased Bruiser to please her by going into the tank, but even at ten he was not much affected by the pathos of fundamentalist Christianity. It was, to him, a lurid, monarchial tale that just didn't apply to the likeable, democratic world that he knew. His church had so protected him from exposure to the fierce, heart-breaking truths of Christianity that Little Bruiser might have defined his religious heritage, had he known he possessed such a thing, as consisting of one part heat and one part bugs.

First Christian Church had no air-conditioning, so from mid-April to mid-October, when Arkansas lids the continental skillet, the congregation worshipped with the windows open, hoping to lure an incautious zephyr into the molten, viscid air of the sanctuary. The sticky heat of the Arkansas summer coated the First Christians like warm varnish; it was a dulling force, made heavier by the drone of sermons and the drag of maudlin hymns which caused old men and bored children to nod, resist, nod, resist, nod, resist, nod, nod, doze.

The only weapon against the heat was the little posterboard hand fan, stapled to a tongue-depressor handle, with a pastel picture of Jesus on the front (usually *The Good Shepherd*) and a terse advertisement on the back for Buie Funeral Home. There were maybe a dozen of these fans scattered among the hymnal racks on the backs of the pews. They were practically

worthless as cooling devices, as Bro. C.T. Steinmetz, the cele-
brated pamphleteer who was called "the great ponderer of
artifacts from pulpit and pew," noted in his tract, *Christ's Fans*:
"To move a noticeable volume of air with one of the stupid
things, you had to pump it harder than you would a churn.
And the effect was never enough even to dry the extra per-
spiration brought on by the extra exertion. They served mainly
as discreet mortuary billboards, of limited practical use except
to give jittery dowagers something to do with their hands."

(Bruiser added this footnote: "Daddy Joe would sometimes
break a splinter off the handle of one of the fans to use, after
taking Holy Communion, as a toothpick.")

Fighting against the heat-induced drowsiness, Little Bruiser
often gazed out through those open windows and envied the
purple martins and swirling cirrus their light and pagan freedom. Sometimes he watched the little girl who lived next
door, pedaling her red tricycle in the deep sycamore shade of
her yard. In that cool cathedral of the open air, she was an
appealing rebuke to the stifling Christian ritual. She entertained herself out there with that marvelous unselfconscious
resourcefulness of solitary children to constantly reshape the
world to suit a fleeting fancy. A big old dog followed her
around, watchful and protective but careful not to intrude
unbidden into that special world she created as she pedaled
along. Bruiser felt drawn to that little girl in the same way he
imagined the dog was. In time he would take the dog's place,
when the little girl grew up to be Scamp.

The open windows at First Christian seldom attracted a
breeze but they always attracted bugs. The most noticeable of
them were a variety of big chocolate-colored rowdy whose
sole function in the ecological scheme was to discombobulate
histrionic preachers; but the *scary* ones were the wasps. They
generally spent their leisure lolling in the sticky dust that
attached to the tops of the globed, pendulous light fixtures that
hung six feet above the pews. When the lights were turned on
for a church service, that greasy dust began to warm and
slicken, and the wasps slowly lost their adhesion and began
an inexorable slide down the prime meridians of those globes.
At the Tropic of Capricorn, they would drop like exiled Satan
into the congregation below. Bro. Steinmetz, in his *Demons In
Disguise*, described the unpleasantness that often ensued:
"In a church thus illuminated, it was 22 mins. after the light
was switched on, give or take a few secs., before the first wasp

fell. By that time, the service was underway. A mood of quiet reverence had been established by means of the call to worship. Usually a prayer was in progress, heads bowed, backs of necks cruelly exposed. One neck always managed to position itself with plumbline precision directly below a light, so the falling wasp couldn't avoid said neck if it tried. So irresistible wasp met immovable neck with a plop, and the instinctive reaction of nape owner was to snap head upright, thus trapping said wasp between medulla oblongata and starched collar. A sting was inevitable, with predictable disruptive consequences.

"Said wasp might then slip farther under said collar, down alarmed and squirming pilgrim's back, and begin stinging pilgrim in hard-to-reach area between the shoulderblades. Said pilgrim might then run amok through the sanctuary, yelling wildly and throwing off various articles of clothing, giving fellow pilgrims the impression of delirium tremens or epileptic seizure. This is thought to be the origin of 'holy-rolling.'

"If said pilgrim were lucky, he might brush away said wasp without getting stung. In that case, he would likely knock the angry creature directly on to the exposed abdomen of a 2-wk.-old hyperallergic infant, or on to the cheek of a fractious attorney given to frivolous seven-digit damage suits. Even when everyone escaped immediate harm, the wasp would then launch a menacing display of aerobatics against which only those evangelists called spellbinders might compete successfully for sinners' attention."

The First Christian elders never called in an exterminator or took systematic anti-wasp measures between services. Maybe that was because they knew that eliminating one batch of wasps would just make room for another the next time the windows were opened. Or maybe it was because the wasp problem wasn't as great as Bruiser and Bro. Steinmetz remembered. Probably, though, it was because of something else that hung over that doughty band of Disciples, something besides the summer heat and the Holy Ghost. The air in that sanctuary was heavy with fatalism. It had an almost Calvinistic authority about it which ruled out all but essential tampering, and it seemed to regard wasps as a natural attendant hazard to the act of worship, if not as actual ordainments providentially scripted into the service for the purpose of counterpoint. If that sounds farfetched, consider this: Bruiser

recalled the night during a summer revival meeting when a
bat flew into the sanctuary along with the bugs, and the
enterprising evangelist made a brilliant extemporaneous
change in his sermon text, so that one who didn't know better
might have supposed that the bat had been specially dis-
patched, like the dove at the baptism of Jesus, to serve as a sort
of theological visual aid.

Bruiser remembered, driving along, some of the weighty
religious discussions he'd had with the Great Travis Shellnut.

"I can just see old Moses," Travis said one time, "standing
there on the mountain, saying to God, 'Now let me get this
straight — You want us to cut the ends of our *peckers* off.'"

Another time Travis got agitated when Bruiser told him
what happened to Lot's wife. "You mean just cause she looked
at her home town burnin' up, God turned 'er into a block of
salt?"

"That's what our preacher said."

"What'd Lot do with 'er after that?"

"I guess he just left 'er there."

"I guess so. Probley too heavy to try and haul off. But looks
like he would've threw a raincoat over 'er, so she wouldn't
melt first time it come up a rain. What'd the preacher say
about that?"

"He didn't say nothin' about it."

"I guess she melted, then. Or all them camels they got over
there licked 'er till there wadn't nothin' left. Why'd God do
something like that?"

"I don't know."

"A lot of what you hear about God," Travis said, "He sounds
like a real rat."

Bruiser later went through that phase in which he had to
work very hard to prove what a depraved and worldly sinner
he was. Once he got past that, he was able to admit that his
religious training at First Christian Church had been good for
him in many ways. It had given him and his family an oasis in
what otherwise would have been a barren social life. By
emphasizing "spiritual" accomplishments, it had given him a
notion of status, raising his appraisal of his self-worth and
giving him a chance to believe in progress. By entempling a
personal God Who knew exactly what He was doing, it had
provided him with an emotional bulwark against the lonely
whispers of individual inadequacy in a time of general chaos.
By imposing on him a decent moral code it had girded him

against being duped by his own cleverness; and if it had cratered his psyche with scar tissue as a result of all the repressions, it had compensated him belatedly by allowing him to look without envy at all the strutters who led all the tacky contemporary parades. Californians especially.

But if that Old Time Religion had been a well-intentioned and even a useful fraud, it hadn't been a harmless one. Leaping back from the fear of death into the arms of the preposterous isn't an evil — unless it deprives a person of his one sure opportunity to discover courage. Wallowing in cheap guilt isn't a crime — unless it muddles a person's understanding of his real responsibility. And Bruiser thought the church had betrayed him on both those counts.

He intended to ask Aunt Laura Bell some hard questions about that.

But Aunt Laura Bell was in one of her gabby moods. She met him at the door of the wisteria-hung little house in Sheridan where she and Uncle Plug had lived for forty years; she directed him to sit in the porch swing while she settled herself in a rocker, and she let him talk for maybe half a minute before she commandeered the conversation for good.

"Lost?" she said. "What would a child like you know about lost. Poor Grover Shale, now *there's* a case of being lost ..."

Grover Shale was Uncle Plug's nephew, which made him some sort of cousin-in-law to Bruiser. Grover had been a hermit from the time Bruiser got old enough to be aware of him. He lived alone in the Lost Creek bottom in a tarpaper shack surrounded by No Trespassing and Keep Out signs. It was said that anyone who approached the shack was greeted with shotgun fire. Grover had a tangle of long stringy hair and a full unkempt beard; his clothes had gradually become filthy rags and he supposedly sustained himself on wild squirrels, farkleberries and rainwater. He shunned all society except for Uncle Plug, who thought it was normal enough for a man to choose such a life, and who drove down to the shack from time to time to check on him.

"... You know Grover's the reason you have such a fear of wasps," Aunt Laura Bell went on. "You were just a baby but I don't doubt for a minute that that's what warped you. Nothing to be ashamed of. Warped me too. I don't mind admitting it. Hateful things scare me silly since that day. I'd flit 'em all day long if I didn't wear out so easy. What good are they? Good for nothing, just like a thousand-legger or one of these old biting flies. Must have been put here for something, but only the Lord knows what. I'd hate to hear what Grover would say about that.

"We never had a shortage of wasps at First Christian, as you know, and we just accepted them as part of the Lord's mysterious will. But the one that dropped in on us that Sunday morning was the biggest, meanest old thing you ever saw. Big red devil, just spoiling for trouble. Kept the congregation nervous through the whole service. Even had to keep one eye open during the prayers.

"Only one didn't notice the wasp was Grover, who was our songleader then. He was inspired with his songleading that morning. Put on a real show with it. Led us in singing four or five hymns, and really pepped up the service by making us sing a verse over again when he thought we hadn't sung it loud enough or sincere enough, and by making the men sing one verse and the women the next and then all join in on the chorus, and other clever things like that. Then he did 'The Old Rugged Cross' for his solo, and it was a moving performance, and after that we all settled back to listen to Brother Belcher's sermon. Brother Belcher was our pastor then, you know.

"I sat there during the sermon thinking about what a fine singer Grover was. A natural-born talent! Voice was deep as a bullfrog's but pure as a mockingbird's. And he *could* carry a tune! His solos were the highlight of the service for years, if you ask me. Sometimes he'd do something touching like 'In The Garden' and sometimes something rich and powerful like 'Were You There When They Crucified My Lord?' In that one, he'd sing 'oh oh oh oh, sometimes it causes me to tremble, tremble, tremble' with such force it would cause *me* to tremble. I could get carried away just watching him up there, so handsome, with his nice wavy hair and big pearly white teeth. He *looked* like a singer, and I heard more than one person remark on how much he resembled Smilin' Joe Roper, the leader of the Melody Boys Quartet. Him being my nephew didn't have a thing to do with this admiration I had for him. You might think it did but it didn't.

"Well, Brother Belcher finally got through boring us to death with his sermon, and signaled Grover to move down front and center, beside the communion table, to lead us in the Hymn of Invitation. Hymn of Invitation that morning was 'Softly and Tenderly.' Grover led us in one verse of it, then paused to let the preacher beg sinners to come forward and give their lives to Jesus Christ. Nobody came, so Grover launched us into the second verse, then paused again to let the preacher beg some more.

"Brother Belcher begged longer and harder than usual that morning because we had visitors with a need-to-be-saved look about them. But they wouldn't come forward, and Grover launched us into the third verse. He gave that one special treatment, hoping to break down the stubborn hearts of those sinners. He was singing as flamboyant as I ever saw him, sweating like Dobbin and all wrapped up in the pretty music and its wonderful message. Wasn't giving a thought in the world to that old wasp. But when he came to the climax of the hymn, the passage that says, 'Come home, come co-o-ome, ye who are weary come ho-o-me,' sweeping his arms like a band conductor and making a grand to-do, the wasp swooped down from the ceiling in a long buzzing dive like a Jap warplane and smacked him right between the eyes.

"Hit him a terrible lick. You could hear it pop. *Whow!,* like a gun going off.

"Stunned Grover. Stunned him a right smart. He staggered back up against the communion table, so dazed he had a upward-looking and awestruck look on his face like you see on the faces of the Apostles in the old religious pictures. He put a hand down on the communion table to support himself, but accidentally knocked over the communion set. All the little communion glasses, some still full of grape juice, clattered and crashed to the floor.

"Collision dazed old Mr. Wasp, too, and I hopped right up from my pew and stomped the sorry rascal. That wasn't a bit ladylike but it just flew all over me what that devil had done to Grover. In all the commotion, Old Man Harry Rubow, deaf as a stick, thought the service was over and got up to leave. The Koon child got scared and started squalling. Brother Belcher turned white as flour and started stammering, 'Get thee behind me, Satan.' Rest of the congregation was shocked silent for a minute, then we rushed up to see about Grover's condition.

"Crowding around him, we could see his forehead was already swelled up like a gourd, and he looked mighty peaked, but he got his wits back and told us he was all right. Then he said, 'I want you people to go back and set down in your pews. Got something I want to say.' We thought that was peculiar on account of Grover didn't sound like his good-natured self.

Sounded mad and impatient, like he was *ordering* us back to our pews. Some of the men didn't appreciate his attitude, but we all took our places. There was considerable mumbling until Grover said, 'All right, now everybody be quiet.' Then he made us a little speech.

"He said, 'Folks, I just want you to know I don't think the Lord had any right to send that wasp in here to attack me like that. I been up here singing my heart out for him for twenty-three year and he didn't have cause to pull a stunt like that on me.'

"That stirred up more mumbling, and I whispered to my husband, Mr. Stuckey: 'Wasp poison done addled Grover's mind.'

"'You might say the Lord didn't have nothing to do with it,' Grover went on. 'But if he can go to the trouble of numbering the hairs on our heads and marking the fall of every mangy sparrow, then he sure ought to be able to keep check on a solitary wasp. No sir, it was the Lord's doing, all right. He sent that demon in here for the purpose of popping me upside the head, and I just don't appreciate it. You might say the Lord's punishing me for my shortcomings, and if that's right, all I can say is the Lord has a poor and regrettable sense of timing — attacking me when I'm up here leading a song that's supposed to bring the lost into his fold. If he was trying to humble me before men, like he done Job, seems like he could have waited till I finished the chorus. It just ain't fair, no way you look at it. No justice in it, period.'

"Well, the more Grover talked, the madder he got, and the madder he got, the more that goose egg on his forehead swole. He was beginning to not even look like a man, with his eyes puffed nearly shut and his face pooching out all over, like a heathen idol or a gruesome face on a totem pole. Brother Belcher couldn't break out of his trance, telling Satan louder and louder to get behind him, but Grover shouted him down, saying, 'Now preacher, let me speak my piece; you get to preach all the time, but this here is my only shot at it.' He finally got Brother Belcher shut up, then went on:

"'It'd be different if I hadn't dedicated my entire adult life to the service of the Lord, glorifying him every way I knowed how. I wasn't a very good Sunday School teacher, I'll admit that. And I wasn't as faithful as I could have been about coming to prayer meeting, but you all know the reason for that, and I don't think you hold it against a man, even if the

Lord *does*, that the railroad makes him work the night shift for a living. I've tithed regular, you can check Miss Erma's ledger books on that. I've worked hard on our visitation program, going into people's homes and trying to talk Jesus to them when I could tell they wished I'd leave so they could go back to watching their TV. Even during the war, when I was in the Marines and the artillery was coming in on us, I witnessed for the Lord every chance I got in the foxholes. Some of them Marines didn't appreciate that, but I done it. I done my part passing the time with the sick and afflicted, and if any of you was ever bedfast and I didn't get around to see you, I'm powerful sorry and ask your forgiveness. I set up thirteen nights running with old Mrs. Clegg when she was dying, and I was proud to do it, 'cause I might be dying in the old folks' home some day and need somebody to set with me. You all know about my songleading, and there's more to that than you realize 'cause there's times when my heart says to me, "Grover, I just don't feel like getting up there and trying for the millionth time to get them folks to sing 'When the Roll Is Called Up Yonder' with a little conviction." And who do you think is responsible for getting the manger scene set up in front of the churchhouse every Christmas? I'll tell you who: Grover Shale, yours truly, who stands before you now with nothing to show for all that work and effort in the Lord's behalf except a pumpknot big as a mushmelon and grapejuice stains all over the britches leg of his only good suit.'

"My husband Mr. Stuckey leaned over and whispered to me, 'That boy's got speaking talent. We ought to run him for county judge.'

"That was a cruel thing to say of someone standing up there with scrambled brains talking nonsense, and I would have told Mr. Stuckey so, except I didn't want to miss any of what Grover was saying.

"He was saying: 'And I'll tell you people something else. I'm tired of playing Santy Claus for our Christmas program every year. It don't fool the children any. The children don't think it's Santy when I come busting out of the pastor's study with that pillow tied around my belly, wearing that silly suit and them cotton whiskers and carrying all them sacks of fruit and nuts and saying, "Ho! Ho! Ho!" They aren't fooled a minute. They say to themselves, "I sure wish old Grover would quit all that foolishness and hurry up and give me my sack." So what's the point of it? There *ain't* no point, folks. It's just a big stupid lot of trouble. But I've gone along with it ten year. And you know why? Not for my sake. Not by a long shot. It's unbearable hot in that Santy suit. And it's hard on a man's pride to have to jump out and go around patting them brats on the head and giving them that manure about reindeers and the North Pole and elfs making toys that they know durn well come out of the Sears and Roebuck catalogue. That's hard on a grown man. But yours truly has done it all these years. Done it as a way of serving the Lord. And now the Lord pays me back by setting out there on his gold throne and saying, "Well, it's a slow day so I think I'll send me an old wasp down there and have him pop old Grover a good one during the Hymn of Invitation." Tell me, is that justice? No sir, it's not. It's just plain not. I think I can claim to have done right by the Lord, and if he's going to act this way, I'm telling you folks here and now that this old boy is through trying to pacify him. You can mark that down.'

"Grover looked to be on the verge of saying something else, but then he got a real disgusted look on his face — at least I *think* it was a disgusted look; it was hard to tell, he was swole up so — and he said, 'Aw, shoot!' Then he tore off up the center aisle and through the vestibule and slammed the front door of the churchhouse behind him.

"I say he 'tore off' up the aisle. What he did, he weaved and wobbled up the aisle, on account of not being able to see plain, I suppose. But even though he stumbled some, you could see he was walking out headstrong and determined and mad as... well, mad as a hornet. His wife Charlene ran out after him, intending to carry him up to see Dr. Jack, but he wouldn't get in the car with her and wouldn't even talk to her. He walked home, packed a few things in his grip, and moved out to that shack in the woods that same afternoon.

"Charlene tried many times to get close enough to talk some sense into him, but all he would do was shoot at her. I had her take *me* down there once, and he shot at both of us. I hated to see him tear up a happy home, and I hated to see him risk hell fire by refusing to come back to church, and I hated to see him waste his wonderful talent. Our hymn-singing at First Christian never was the same without him. But I wasn't going to get *shot* over it. One time of dodging buckshot was enough for me.

"I hoped that my husband Mr. Stuckey could get him to see the light, but you might know hardheaded Mr. Stuckey *agreed* with him. He goes down to visit him every two or three weeks and always comes back in a cheerful mood. All I can figure is that him and Grover have built them a moonshine still."

CHAPTER TWENTY-ONE

Roots

It also became fashionable around this time to look for oneself among one's roots. Bruiser made some discreet genealogical inquiries, but found only two ancestors who interested him much.

One was John Sevier, who gets a respectful nod in the history texts as the first governor of Tennessee. Like Bruiser, John Sevier had an unusual name put on him after he was a grown man. He was called Nolichucky Jack. The name sounds faintly amusing to the modern ear, as though it might have derived from some incident involving vomiting and pancakes, but it's doubtful that any of Jack's coonskin contemporaries laughed at his name or made fun of his vomiting, because he had a short fuse and liked to hoist his piece.

Nolichucky Jack was one of those peripheral historical characters who are so entertaining in their lively disreputability that conscientious historians neglect or sanitize them lest they outshine the important clods and posthumously corrupt the impressionable. He was a legendary figure of the Colonial Era frontier, the dashing shoot-'em-up leader of rough mountain men from the wild side of the Blue Ridge. He became a hero of the American Revolution when he and his boys Conged the British at the Battle of King's Mountain; but he soon became a public menace when he talked his neighbors into seceding from North Carolina and forming the State of Franklin. With Jack as its governor, Franklin lasted three years, not giving much of a damn what the Carolina dandies and Continental Congressmen with their periwigs and silk britches thought of the arrangement. Legal tender in Franklin was otter pelts and whiskey.

After savaging the British, Jack and his Franklin followers entertained themselves by savaging the neighboring Cherokees. Then Jack got nose deep in a land swindle which the historian Marquis James called "of Napoleonic magnitude," but he never quite went under despite Judge Andrew Jackson's vigorous prosecutorial efforts, and when Franklin got lumped into the new territory of Tennessee and admitted to the union, Jack took the governorship almost as a consolation prize.

He and Jackson became bitter political rivals, and they annoyed one another with such adept and deliberate persistence that a duel probably was inevitable. It was Jackson who sent the challenge — after a public cussfight that Jack had got the better of by razzing Jackson for wife-stealing. Jack, by now an old man, tried his best to ignore the gauntlet that Young Hickory had thrown down. He wondered why Jackson had to be so humorless about these things. Jackson pressed the challenge, and went so far as to publish a public notice in which he declared "that his excellency John Sevier ... is a base coward and poltroon." Still, Jack dallied. This was not at all like him. He was obviously undergoing some crisis of self-doubt. Either that or he was struggling against some latter-day revelation concerning the folly of otherwise sensible men shooting guns at one another over inane and puerile pronunciamentos. Maybe, after having fought thirty-five battles as a younger man, he had achieved enough wisdom in his maturity to be scared shitless of this young zealot who indeed would soon gun down another political opponent in a duel; maybe he had learned enough about life to resolve that he wasn't about to get his gonads shot off or his brains blown out just because Andrew Jackson couldn't take a joke.

In any case, Jackson soon announced that he was removing to the killing ground to await the appearance of his craven excellency. Jack waited five days before skulking upon the scene, still oppressed by a sense of the absurdity of it all, or by something, since Jackson couldn't persuade him to stand still and be shot like a man. Their "duel" quickly deteriorated from dragoons to walking sticks to a new round of yellow-belly name-calling. At one point, Jack hid from Jackson behind a tree! All of this was so unheard-of that it was considered by the mountaineers of early Tennessee to be an aberration of nature — an occurrence so contrary to common knowledge and good sense that it simply did not count in their assessment of ordinary reality — and so neither man's reputation or political fortunes suffered as a result.

There continued to be bad blood between the two families, however, until 1946, when Nolichucky Jack and Old Hickory appeared together on a three-cent U.S. postage stamp that had a conciliatory look about it.

The other Bruiser ancestor was a man whose descendants forgot his legal name. He would be remembered, like Bruiser, only by his nickname, which was One-Eye. One-Eye actually had two eyes and they both worked just fine, but One-Eye was politically ambitious on the local level, and it was thought to be politically advantageous in rural Arkansas during the Gilded Age to be either handicapped or a war veteran, preferably both; and with no war experience One-Eye took to wearing an eye patch while campaigning in the hope of winning some of the more gullible sympathy vote. This tactic didn't work, and One-Eye lost several elections in the drowsy decade before the sinking of the *Maine.*

The eruption of the Spanish-American War allowed him to enlist and become a genuine war vet, and thereafter he dispensed with the eye patch, alleging to those who asked a miracle eye restoration by some faith healer or carnival mountebank; but even with both eyes obviously functioning while he whooped his spiels from the stump, One-Eye continued to be called One-Eye.

He spent the war wasting away with what was then called "swamp fever" in a military camp in Georgia, but nobody in Sheridan knew that, and when he got home he promptly announced that on the strength of his "war record" he was going to run for Grant County jailer. The jailer's job was one of the courthouse plums in those days, in that it provided steady undemanding work and tolerated petty graft and considerable nepotism. The jailer could hire his wife to cook meals for prisoners, his daughter to clean cells, his son to keep records, and so on. One-Eye had little to recommend him for such an important office, but he had a new speech, which he saved to unveil during the big "speaking" that was always held on the courthouse square in Sheridan on the eve of the election. The speech not only got him elected, it got him elected by a landslide, almost by acclamation, and insured him a lifetime career in county politics.

No record of the famous speech survives, but according to family tradition, this is what One-Eye said:

"You folks have heard many accounts of what happened in the late war, but I was privileged to be there, and if you want to hear the eyewitness truth of the matter, give heed.

"The outcome was still in doubt until one day me and Teddy are settin' on our hosses down at the bottom of this-ere San Jew-wan Hill. We're settin' there bushed from the unendin' weeks of constant combat, the likes of which not even Bedford Forrest ever saw. I'm talkin' tired, folks. I mean, we'd give it just about all the heroic effort that was in us. Settin' there wore to a frazzle, but then I turn and look at Teddy and he turns and looks at me, and he says, Teddy does, 'One-Eye, looks like we'll just have to take this old hill, no gettin' around it.' I says, 'Well sir, it won't be took without a cost, but I reckon you're right — this hill's the key to it, and it's got to be took.'

"Teddy, he goes to mullin' our chances, which he calculates as just fair, and while he's mullin', I take a nip of corn and a gnaw of my quid and give my nag a right smart of a spur and thunder off up that hill, yellin' like one of Mosby's banshees. Teddy, he comes right on my flank, and the boys fall in behind us and up that hill we charge.

"It was a sight to stir the heart of every true niece and nephew of Uncle Sam, them brave boys fallin' and dyin' all around, enrichin' that greaser soil with their good red American blood. Well sir, we fight up that hateful old hill a yard, two yards at a time, shootin' and saberin' right and left, punchin' through the enemy ranks, through the balls and smoke and corpses and bayonets, and finally we break through. Halleleujah, we turn the tide and put the bloody Spaniard on the run.

"We scratch and claw our way to the top of that dirty dog of a hill, and when we get to the summit, we chop us a pole and we run up Old Glory. Yes sir, there it was, tattered by grapeshot and scorched by musket powder, but wavin' high and proud over the whole Caribbean. And all them maimed and sufferin' boys raises such a cheer that the cold-hearted tyrant settin' on his gold throne in Madrid must have heard it and shivered. It was the grandest moment I ever been privileged to be a part of, and we all knew what a grand day it was for our country.

"In fact, as we set there on our nags, our hearts on fire with patriotic pride, Teddy turns to me and says, 'One-Eye, us takin' this-ere hill was one of the grand moments in the history of our country.' I rolled my chaw into my cheek and spit and I says, 'Yes sir, Teddy, I reckon it was.'

"Teddy, he mulls that for a spell, then he says, 'It was *such* a grand moment in our history, One-Eye, that me or you one is goin' back home and get elected President of the United States because of it.'

"Now it was *my* turn to mull, and I mulled over what he had said, rolled my quid a time or two, looked up at Old Glory wavin' there in the tropical breeze. I spit, then I says, 'Yes sir, Teddy-boy, I reckon you're right about that, too. But I tell you what. *You* be the president, Teddy. All I want is to go back home and get elected Grant County jailer.'"

CHAPTER TWENTY-TWO

A Squatter in Longfellow's Yard

When Bruiser got an invitation to spend a year at Harvard University, filling in the few gaps that Frog Level had left in his higher education, he wasn't sure he should go. Harvard had turned out one president who had treated members of Bruiser's profession to the Alien and Sedition Acts, and another who had engineered the madness that had killed Travis Shellnut in a jungle nine thousand miles from home. It had turned out Cotton Mather and Timothy Leary and Henry Kissinger and John Kenneth Galbraith, who had recently penned a truly embarrassing account of his ill-starred infatuation with the actress Angie Dickinson. That didn't seem a healthy environment for an impressionable young man who was lost enough already.

But the place was said to be close to Walden Pond, and close to the ocean, which Bruiser had seen only once as a child but which had somehow always called to him; and he'd be able to hobnob with famous anthropologists and economists and geneticists and such, whose grandiose interpretations of human existence might give him some clues to modestly interpreting his own. So he hauled Scamp and the young'uns to Boston and they spent an academic year lodged in a horizontal tenement that defiled what had once been Henry Wadsworth Longfellow's front lawn.

Bruiser found Harvard to be a better college, by and large, than Frog Level A&M had been. Instead of modern dance and speech, it taught him Chinese and law, and it introduced him to some of the social graces unknown in Arkansas. The sophisticated expression of enthusiasm, for example, which he learned while watching a World Series game on TV in the Faculty Club with an old professor of classics who kept stifling whoops and hot-damns but finally couldn't contain his excitement, and shouted, "By Jove, those Orioles are indefatigable!" Or the proper attire for a formal reception: His first invitation to one of these included the notation, "Medals may be worn." Bruiser didn't have any silver stars lying around, and the closest thing to a medal that he could find in his poke was an "Eat More Possum" lapel pin that his brother Bill had given him once, so he wore that. Only after arriving at the reception did he learn that the reference was to medals awarded by the king of Sweden to winners of the Nobel Prize.

Bruiser rightly supposed that this Harvard sojourn might be his last best chance to find his authentic self through education. So between extended periods of lying dopily on the bank of the river Chiles watching scullers row by, and perching lazily on the promontory above Marblehead watching the sailboats in the blue harbor, he studied hard. He tried like Thomas Wolfe to read all ten million books in the library, and he paid attention as the old professorial lions bearded one another in their classroom dens. He thought he might be making progress. But in the end he came to agree with Thoreau that maybe Massachusetts and Arkansas didn't have much to communicate. It was stimulating, all right, the rarefied Harvard air that ruined Emerson and Henry Adams and killed Quentin Compson; but Bruiser never learned to breathe it easily. He missed the bayou air of home, that humid soup of loblolly and muscadine, of whippoorwill and cypress shadow, that made the night so fine and ghosty driving along levee roads with the car window rolled down, listening to Garner Ted Armstrong and Del Rio, Texas, on the radio. He missed cornbread, and sorry old dogs barking at the moon, and frogs, and people who threatened to whip his ass for what he said he believed and then wanted to buy him a Co-cola at the Dairy Queen later on, without either of them having changed opinions or given ground. The Harvard nostrum was that at Cambridge a man could finally *think* his way clear to salvation, but Bruiser was too much a whirling up of alluvial dirt and niggersong and poolhall poetry ever to put much stock in so unsouthern and unjesus a proposition.

Harvard was as lost in its own way as Bruiser was. The ferment of the Sixties had already gone flat everywhere else, drugged out or drained off into rock music and casual sex and Newspeak politics and cult movements and petty crime, but Cambridge was still a redoubt for true believers. They were legion — the old libs who had been ploughhorses for the New Deal or knights at Kennedy's Camelot, and all their bright young associates, all convinced that the late campus disorders had set the stage for some colossal liberating upheaval, which they would serve as academic theoreticians and apologists. Bruiser heard so much of this, spoken so fervently, that he sold all his stock in all the capitalist-pig corporations — or would have if he'd owned any.

One night at Harvard Bruiser traipsed through the snow to attend a "lecture" by Norman Mailer, who was this phantom revolution's pet prophet, having declared that the fighting in the streets wouldn't abate for forty years. This lecture turned out to be the unveiling of a stupid pornographic movie that Mailer had made, and the prophet looked fat and drunk and lost. Whatever his movie was supposed to signify, it was not revolution — actually, it was just an embarrassment — and the signs and portents of revolution were just as unpersuasive everywhere else on the campus all through the year. Hardcore remnants of once-feared radical organizations slouched a-round trying to stir some interest in a boycott against some oil company, and when Nixon invaded Cambodia, they broke a few shopkeepers' windows as a way of showing their moral indignation, but that was about it. When a cadre "occupied" the administration building, the bureaucrats took an un-scheduled holiday and the siege ended after a couple of days without anyone having much noticed.

This wasn't the cutting edge of a revolution; it was table scraps from Alice's Restaurant, and Bruiser looked it over and was slightly terrified to realize that the brightest people of his time didn't know any more than he did what to make of the fact that, whatever else they might be, they were trapped in dying animals. Insofar as he could tell, their "revolution" was something of a low-budget Second Coming, with the sheep and goats redesignated ideologically, and probably with the phantasmagoria reduced to simple gore, but with roughly the same likelihood of coming anon to pass.

Maybe every generation is the Lost Generation. Bruiser's was the one that had come of age between the Squares and the Hippies, between the gray flannel suit and love beads, and it was Veritas fashion for Bruiser to sit around brooding over whether he had been born too early or too late. Here's what he concluded:

Too young to have been smeared by Joe McCarthy, he was already too old and ornery to let himself be pied-pipered by Gene. Too young for the music and ideology of Peekskill, he was too broadmoored and taiwaned to be lured by the music and nihilism of Woodstock. He had barely missed the Depression that shaped one generation and the Vietnam obsession that warped another. His generation, with nothing else to occupy it, had taken the role of assuming the blame for everything that the other generations were angry or disillusioned or disgruntled about. Bruiser had accepted that role even while renouncing it. November 22, 1963, had to be *some*body's fault, so Bruiser let it be his. The Assassination, and all the later ones, were the result of some deep-seated Bruiser character flaw, the same one that caused My Lai, Wounded Knee, Auschwitz, the atom bomb, racism, pollution and ten thousand and five dead mosquitoes. The need to expiate some of the gratuitous guilt was why he tended to identify with the troublemaking side in most of the social skirmishes that were his era's chief entertainment. But those sympathies didn't lighten his load. If anything, they only made him feel guilty that he had never looted an appliance store during a riot.

Whenever someone, no matter who, said, "If you're not part of the solution, you're part of the problem," Bruiser knew they were talking about him.

As with Leonard Bernstein and Tom Wicker, those pangs led Bruiser to think and say some mighty silly things.

"Why couldn't it have been *me* that got shot?" he said to Scamp after the Kent State massacre.

Scamp considered that an absurd remark and told him so.

"I don't mean *killed*," he said. "Wounded, maybe. Not just a scratch or nick, though. I mean a wound serious enough to matter. Not one that would turn me into a vegetable or anything, but serious enough so I could speak with moral authority on the subject, whatever the subject is. Like Orwell getting shot in the throat at Catalonia. After that, when he wrote about the Spanish Civil War, nobody could sneer at him and say, 'What do *you* know about it, Limey? Where were *you* when the bullets whined?' You know what I'm saying?"

"'Give me liberty or give me a flesh wound'," Scamp said.

Was that what he was saying? He didn't mean to be saying that. He didn't intend to trivialize Kent State or the other epochal encounters. He was only regretting that it seemed his destiny to be a mere spectator as his little float paraded by. By keeping his professional and generational and temperamental distance, he had missed his chance to ride in the parade. His credentials as a journalist made his non-involvement respectable, but if his work might make him the eyes and ears of history, he would never be history's voice or fist. He'd never be a Yankee as long as he was damn old Mel Allen.

Once or twice he'd been a bruise collector at the barricades. A state trooper had knocked him cold with a nightstick at a sit-in against racial segregation at Little Rock; and in Washington D.C., he had been gassed, maced and dragged away from the Washington Monument by the police during a Fourth of July come-ye-all. But those hadn't been blood sacrifices that mattered, as getting shot at Kent State or lynched at Selma would have mattered. In both cases, he had become a casualty in the line of duty, involuntarily and quite by accident, as Lou Costello might have, and both times had tried as cravenly as he knew how to extricate himself unharmed.

"Hey! Hold on! Wait! It's *them* you want to club, not me."

No, Bruiser didn't want to die or bleed or even get hot and sweaty for any of the great social causes that kept his country in turmoil in the years between the Assassination and the Resignation. He wasn't one of the ones who would find his voice and his identity at the barricades; he was no more convincing in fatigues than Patty Hearst or Castro; no more of a revolutionary than any of the other would-be radicals who gathered around the prophet's projector to witness the end of a fantasy.

CHAPTER TWENTY-THREE

O De Doo Dah Day

Bruiser expected the worst when circumstances required him to move to the city of Philadelphia, in the commonwealth of Pennsylvania, but the smart set there met him with open arms. He and Scamp had hardly got their poke off the flatbed when their first engraved invitation arrived. It wasn't from Princess Grace's folks or Eugene Ormandy, but it *was* Main Line and old money. His and Scamp's presence was requested at one of the most exclusive of the suburban country clubs. This club discriminated not only against blacks, Jews, proles and the ordinary vulgar rich; it also excluded anyone who had ever been known to ride in the front seat of a car. One of its membership requirements was that the applicant not know that there was United States currency with portraits on it other than those of Woodrow Wilson and Salmon P. Chase. Bruiser would never have been considered for admission, but the club wished praise in the public prints for its philanthropy, so it stooped to ask Bruiser to one of its annual lavish soirees, a charity ball, in order to take notes for a newspaper encomium.

"Imagine," Bruiser told Scamp, "someone who grew up in a sharecropper shack nibbling caviar and doing the minuet and standing around deploring welfare chiselers with the real pros."

"You didn't grow up in a *shack*," Scamp said.

"Compared to this bunch I did," Bruiser told her.

There was still in Bruiser something of the plump little peasant suspecting that fulfillment might lie in social climbing, so he was determined that they would attend this affair and spare no ostentation. He rented a tuxedo, and Scamp, in the manner of Scarlett O'Hara, improvised a fetching ballgown from some garage-sale gleanings. The shirt that came with the tux was too small in the neck, but Bruiser realized that a degree of discomfort went with the pleasures of haut monde and he gave up on the shirt only after Scamp convinced him that her lavender gown would clash with his purple face. A dapper colleague agreed to lend him a larger-necked dress shirt in return for Bruiser's solemn vow to open a vein if he dribbled champagne on the ruffles. Bruiser had never been in a limousine other than the airport type, but he worked out a deal with an acquaintance, a newspaper's obituary writer who knew a mortuary employee who owed him a favor. This undertaker's helper agreed to "borrow" a funeral-home limo for the evening and to livery himself as its driver in a uniform belonging to a Bellevue Stratford bellhop, who owed *him* a favor. All of this wound up costing Bruiser an arm and a leg — well, eighty-five dollars — but as he told Scamp, how often did one get to rub fetlocks with the Philadelphia horsey set?

It turned out to be horsier than he had imagined. The invitation had said something about the "theme" of the event being that of a "Horseless Horse Show," but Bruiser and Scamp didn't know what that meant and didn't think about it again until they arrived at the clubhouse, where they were greeted by a butler or doorman who neighed at them.

He neighed at them like a horse.

Bruiser didn't know quite what to make of that. He shot a quick glance at Scamp, who seemed just as perplexed although unperturbed. Having had no experience with such things, he assumed that it was traditional for butlers or doormen at such events to meet arriving guests with a neigh, and not wanting to appear gauche, he responded with a hearty neigh of his own.

He neighed again when, inside, the hat-check girl greeted him and Scamp with a robust filly whinny.

Having successfully handled those peculiar preliminaries with the hired help, Bruiser was eager to get on into the ballroom and mingle with some Beautiful People. And he and Scamp were hardly through the door when they bumped into their first aristocrats. This was a couple who certainly looked the part — a buxom matron, aglitter with diamonds and sequins, and her debonair escort in black tie and tails, with the dignified bearing of an Averell Harriman. Probably Wentworths or Graybills, Bruiser thought, remembering his John O'Hara, and he was prepared to be abashed by their casual elegance.

But at the moment the Wentworths or Graybills were involved in an activity so amazing that Bruiser forgot to feel outclassed. The missus was astraddle her dignified gentleman's back and hanging on like a bronc-rider — more like a kangaroo-rider, actually — and he was doing his best to canter around the room in the stately manner of one of the Budweiser Clydesdales. He was having quite a time keeping his poise, outweighed by his rider by at least three stone, and he staggered slightly, Atlas-like, on his turns. He didn't say anything to Bruiser and Scamp; he only rolled his eyes, horse-like, while his rider emitted a thin but delighted titter, something on the order of a roller-coaster *wheeeee!*

Bruiser's first thought was that he and Scamp had walked in on one of the great all-time faux pas of Philadelphia high society. These poor socialites probably had devoted their lives to winning and maintaining a place here among the elite, and now, perhaps because of too many early-evening slurps at the champagne trough, they were making a scene that would scandalize the club and cause them to live out their days in rueful disgrace. Pity!

But on recovering from his momentary astonishment, Bruiser looked around and found that this wasn't the only couple making horses of themselves. Nearby, a Dior-ed heiress was leading her squire around with some velvet "reins," and he paused just in front of Bruiser to paw the floor communicatively, the way Trigger always did when he wanted to tell Roy something. Just beyond them, a quartet of dowager equestriennes were putting their cobs through a steeplechase competition. The men were down on all fours, swaybacked from all the sidesaddle avoirdupois they were bearing, popping studs and ripping cummerbunds right along.

Bruiser didn't know what to think.

"Am I hallucinating?" he asked Scamp in a discreet aside.

"If you are, I wish you'd left me out of it," Scamp said.

They edged around the "arena" — past the "polo field" and the "fox chase," in which Reynaud was exuberantly and repeatedly tallyhoed — and found an out-of-the-way place behind the hors d'oeuvre table. From there Bruiser looked out across this grand spectacle and thought that there was much to be learned here about the march of human civilization. The cultural imagination of the West reached something of a pinnacle here. It was such an awesome display that no amount of jotting down notes could have summarized or memorialized it, and in the end Bruiser scribbled only one: "Is there a Horse Anti-Defamation League?" He would have written more, but he was overcome by the alarming thought that Scamp, who knew her way around Vanity Fair better than he did, might get into the spirit and impulsively leap aboard his withers and spur him snorting and bucking out among all the prancing and preening stallions and mares.

"You know how I'd feel?" he said. "Like the token mule."

"What?" she said.

"Nothing."

"Why don't we go somewhere and get a pizza?" she said.

"In our limousine?"

"Why not?"

That was what he wanted to do, too, but he found himself dallying. He had invested some kind of naive hope in this affray, to say nothing of eighty-five dollars, and he meant to get *some*thing out of it. If one of these jowly old dames lassoed, bulldogged, and hogtied some spry old robber-baron buckaroo, and sizzled her coat-of-arms on his old ham with a branding iron, Bruiser wanted to be around to see it.

"Let's at least guzzle some of the bubbly," he said.

While they guzzled, they watched the show with a continuing sense of wonder.

"Caligula named his horse consul," Bruiser said, "but this is better than that."

"If we'd brought a camera," Scamp said, "we could get rich selling the negatives back to these people when they sober up."

Bruiser loaded a saltine with a big glob of pate de foie gras for the chauffer. Nobody would mind his leaving with a cache of hors d'ouevres, he decided, so long as he let the apples and sugar cubes be.

CHAPTER TWENTY-FOUR

Envoi

Bruiser liked the *idea* of nature as much as Goethe or Thoreau, as much as the organic gardeners and white-water canoeists who were so abundant in his day and time, but as a practical matter he preferred no-iron shirts and spray deodorants and apples and tomatoes without worms in them. He would have preferred a nature with such qualities as sharklessness, snakelessness, wasplessness; one in which there were more Wordsworth cuckoos and fewer Hitchcock crows. He wasn't afraid of nature so much as he just didn't trust it.

This wary view of nature derived from a few dark events of Bruiser's otherwise happy childhood. There was the time that Daddy Joe decided Little Bruiser was old enough to take along on a Saline River fishing trip. That meant Bruiser had to wade off into the snaky, stagnant waters of a roadside barrow pit with one end of the seine in which they caught their fish-bait crawdads. When a big old water moccasin slid off into the water not far from where Little Bruiser was standing hip-deep, D.J. said: "Aw, that old rascal won't bother you, you're ten times bigger'n him." Just then a large crawfish slipped down into Little Bruiser's oversized rubber boot, looped his ankle, and grabbed hold of his big toe with a pincer. Little Bruiser naturally thought the deadly cottonmouth was fanging him, and his horror was such that he lost consciousness. His brothers told him later that he shot straight up out of the water, as if geysered by some unnatural cartoon propulsion, and scrambled laterally, across thin air, fifteen feet to dry safe ground. It was a miracle, they said. A violation of the inviolable laws of physical science. D.J. was not impressed. "How can we seine crawdeads if all you want to do is play in the water?" he said.

It wasn't long after that when Daddy Joe decided that Little Bruiser was old enough to go deer hunting for the first time. He armed the boy with the old family hand-me-down ten-gauge shotgun, which was taller and weighed more than Bruiser did, and would undoubtedly have broken his shoulder with the recoil if he had ever been so foolish as to attempt to shoot it. Bruiser was apprehensive about the deer hunt, but it produced no trauma, only misery and boredom. They were in the unwelcoming December woods before daybreak, and as the gray winter dawning crept through the forest, a sleet's-breath wind blew through Little Bruiser like he was screen wire. There was nothing to do out there, waiting for Bambi, except to shudder and listen to the acorns fall. D.J. had told him that it was essential to be quiet and still, and Little Bruiser wanted to honor the ancient rules. But the brutal cold and accumulating tedium wore down his ten-year-old's resolve after the longest hour since Joshua immobilized the sun.

Daddy Joe was a good hunter but not a fanatical one, and just when Little Bruiser thought he was going to have to break down and whine, the old man said the hell with all those uncooperative deer and set about building a fire. Never one to do things halfway, D.J. didn't just gather a few twigs and start a little tease of a blaze; he set the woods on fire. The whole glade was soon a roaring inferno. He admired it for a time, then strode off toward the pickup. "Come on, Buck," he said cheerfully, "let's go home and get Momma to make us some biscuits." D.J. lived such a charmed life that even forest fires couldn't resist him; he knew this one would die out after charring only an insignificant ten or twelve acres, and it did.

Such encounters tended to deafen Bruiser, as he got older, to the call of the wild. He gave up hunting and fishing even before his chance discovery in Munchkin Manor of the principle of reverence for life. His work allowed him to Saran Wrap himself in an ever more artificial world — a world of floors and pavement rather than ground, or cars and buildings rather than rocks and trees, of conditioned air rather than weather, of television rather than the night sky. His routines were governed by vacuous ideas and contrived events — "news" — rather than by naturally occurring conditions. His relationships with other people were a tangle of abstractions — money, fidelity, homework, recreation — and his environment was a mobile Astrodome shielding him from the elements of chance by which Nature tests the fitness of her hatchlings to survive. Bruiser had no major grievances against this sedentary, indoor life. But in this era of Good Feelings between the Nixon pall and the Carter malaise, nature was much in fashion, even in the city, where Bruiser worked and where the few little outcroppings of nature were mostly mugger-cover or latrines for Rittenhouse dogs. Taxi drivers and traffic cops had their "earthshoes" and organic gardens; Wentworths and Graybills talked of buying Winnebegos and camping out; and a progressive politician had the nerve to tell the press: "I support your so-called ecology one hunnerd per cent."

Ecology, Bruiser thought, might be the last bandwagon. What did he have to lose by climbing aboard?

"I'm going out today to re-establish diplomatic relations with the natural world," he told Scamp one Saturday morning at breakfast. "You want to come along?"

"No thanks," said Scamp, who already had plans to spend the day among the fronds and fountains of the nearby enclosed shopping mall.

Bruiser motored out to a little "wilderness park" that the Taiwan developers had deemed unsuitable for an extension of the subdivisions that circumscribed it; it was no more wilderness than a turnpike median; no more a true expression of nature than modern-day Walden Pond. But Bruiser adjudged it to be closer to nature than the zoo and the attendant told him he wasn't likely to come across anything that would maul or gore him, even if he inadvertently stepped on its tail. The main attraction of the place was a "nature trail," a broad comfortable path about a kilometer long hacked out for the strolling convenience of artificial men in their doubleknit slacks and shined shoes. The trees and shrubs along the path wore handy identification tags, like delegates at a convention, and there were discreet signs pointing the way down twisting side trails to a beaver pond, a bat cave, and a den tree with a hive of honeybees.

It was a fine autumn day, the air as sharp and clean as pine needles, and as Bruiser sauntered along he soon convinced himself that he was back in nature's good graces, as much a part of this woodland as his Choctaw ancestors had been. It was only a pretend wilderness but there was much here to consider: there were wild asters and vines rich with purple berries; there were the eerie cries of woodpeckers and the animated gossip of squirrels; and the red death of the sumac and the miracle of the cocoon. The autumn light itself was remarkable, laying like gold lacquer on the cedar boughs and falling in bright splotches through the doomed deciduous canopy, illuminating octagonal spider webs and the blue transparent wings of drowsing dragonflies, obscuring in the deep shadows a myriad of living shapes and unnumbered unseen eyes. Nature watched him warily through all those unseen eyes. He felt solitude with no other people around, but because of those eyes he never felt quite alone.

Could the eyes be the same ones, he asked himself, that had watched Penn from the same green shadows three centuries before. The yellow eyes of panthers, then called tygers, or the eyes of wolves, reading the future with a tragic intelligence. The eyes of chimerical Indians, always just one silent step beyond seeing. Or might they be eyes as old and as penetrating as those of the wooly mammoth?

No, the eyes would be smaller and stranger now, not so fierce and not so kind. The stick eyes of the mantis and the hairy multiple eyes of the bumblebee. The haunted eyes of the field mouse. The masked eyes of the raccoon. But Bruiser couldn't shake off the creepy notion that they were the old knowing eyes. What was it that they knew? Who did they think they were watching? Did they see him as the diplomat, or did they see, lurking under the threads and the grooming, an old terror, who had belonged here once but was now unwelcome; who kept this place as a walled prison, attempted escape punishable by speeding and screeching death? Bruiser tried to look back at them through the eyes of Fabre, or the eyes of Audubon, or Jack the Slapper, reformed and redeemed: through the eyes of anyone they would accept: an envoi. The thought stole upon him eerily, like fog: could it be that the eyes that were out there watching him were his own? In these green shadows where the old god Time was monarch, immortal and capricious, had the real Bruiser long ago taken refuge from all the dualities and paradoxes, and was it that original and elusive Puck Bruiser who now warily watched Doubleknit Bruiser galoomphing around out here in the dead leaves?

Bruiser sensed that he was close to something here.

But then the moment was gone. The eyes, if they had been

out there, turned away and were gone. Bruiser looked around and discovered he had strayed from the nature trail. He was in a castle of tall evergreens lit by shafts of golden sunlight which sliced down through the canopy from different quadrants of the sky. He was quite turned around, and as he clambered through the underbush searching for the trail, limber branches whipped at him and thorns snatched at his cuffs. A yellowhammer flew by with a hostile scream, and squirrels pelted him with acorns as if in settlement of an old, old score. When he found the trail again, it had the molted skin of a large snake lying across it.

Bruiser went back to that park several times but never again sensed that he was on the verge of a reconciliation of some sort. He didn't feel that he was being watched. He found the evergreen grove again with no trouble, but there was no magic in it, only bits of debris left by thoughtless picnickers. He saw no other snake signs, and the birds and squirrels kept their distance. He interpreted this to mean that nature was challenging him to a bolder initiative, and he was game.

He made plans for a *Deliverance*-type float trip, an excursion that he hoped would be an incursion, and one that included camping out along the way with the mud turtles under the stars.

"You know what Pascal said," Bruiser told Scamp. "'Rivers are roads that take us where we want to go.'"

"Where *you* want to go," she said.

Bruiser invited Bruiser Jr. along.

"No way," said Bruiser Jr., who was twelve. "I'm not going out there and have a bear eat me."

"There's not any bears out there."

"That's what this man thought that was in this *Reader's Digest* true-life adventure. Boy, did he get surprised."

"I promise there won't be any bears."

"That's what you said about dogs on Halloween that time."

"I wouldn't go any place where I couldn't take a shower before I went to bed," his sister Scampette said.

"You could take a shower like the Indians did. Under a waterfall. Wouldn't that be great?"

"Ha! And have a jellyfish fall on my head and sting me to death."

"Rivers don't have jellyfish."

"What about eels, then?"

"Eels?"

"A waterfall would be too cold," their mother said. "You couldn't turn on the hot."

In the end the only boating partner he could recruit was a politician who needed a new campaign gimmick. They scheduled a flatboat run that would allow the candidate to stop and greet voters on photogenic bridges, but they had to cut the trip short because of bad weather. If they'd had good sense they would have called it off, but they let Lewis and Clark and the campaign public relations man get the best of them, and they made a soppy downriver scurry, bailing water and dratting heartless Boreas. They oared past the fogbound state capital before the rain and cold and darkness obliged them to pitch camp on a muddy strand. The blowing rain and a constant canopy of steam kept them from seeing any stars. They wondered about that steam until the next morning, when they returned home rheumy and febrile, soon after waking to find themselves tented at the base of one of the nuclear cooling towers on Three Mile Island.

That was in November, and that blowing rainstorm presaged an early winter. Bruiser had barely recovered from the nuclear night out when his work demanded that he make a quick trip to the shore. When he glimpsed the sea for the first time since the summer, nature whispered another dare, and he stopped the car, stripped to his Fruit of the Loom, and plunged headfirst into the North Atlantic, which was so cold that icebergs had been reported offshore. The water numbed him so quickly that he was unable to swim back to the sand. He had to wait for the rising tide to spit him ashore, along with the broken shells and other flotsam. All he got from that experience was an ear infection that lingered into the new year.

He drove to Valley Forge on a silver afternoon in January, when a heavy snow was on the ground. It was the snow that lured him, and it was beautiful there, glistening in the winter sun that slanted across the upland fields of the mountains named Joy and Misery, capping the lichened boulders and drifting into picturesque configurations along the banks of Valley Creek. It was so pretty he regretted he hadn't brought a camera along.

He cursed his Kodak mentality, his postcard imagination.

How could he ever see picture-pretty snow as an enemy?

He had been thinking about that — about nature as adversary; about Hobbes' nature rather than Rousseau's. In her friendlier moods, nature doesn't teach us much about ourselves. When she's coy and charming, subtle and benign, we let ourselves be dazzled and intrigued by her, amazed and entertained — too bewitched to make useful notes or learn any lessons. Only when she turns hard and mean does she require us to draw on those hidden resources by which we are finally defined.

The contest here hadn't been one of ragged militiamen against nature, or even militiamen against nature's snow. Snow was just the medium through which nature allowed them to confront themselves. They didn't conquer nature; they conquered doubt; they conquered the frittering away of their essential selves into trivial fragments of personality; in short they achieved for themselves exactly what they achieved for their army, and in a larger sense, for their country. And they were able to do it because nature here wasn't shackled or muzzled as she was in a prison park or a neutered river, so she could arrange a challenge that wasn't one of wits but of will. And she wrote it in the stark simple script of snow.

"Well, the snow's still here, and so am I."

With that thought, Bruiser parked the car, removed his shoes and socks, and started walking through the kneehigh snow across one of those broad mountain fields. He walked a hundred yards before he stopped and asked himself who he thought he was kidding. He couldn't make snow his enemy. He couldn't project the momentary sting and ache in his tootsies over four months and through chronic frostbite and gangrene. He couldn't transform this pretty snow into such a primal enemy that he would move his bowels beside his bed inside his hut to avoid putting his frozen feet in it on a midnight trudge to the latrine. People of his time and place didn't have primal enemies. If they had enemies at all, they were enemies created by their own ingenuity or hatched inside their heads. There was no Satan and no Christ to invigorate and ennoble the human struggle for clarification and purpose.

Up ahead, at the crest of the slope, was a battalion of picnic tables. Bruiser didn't think he had ever seen so many picnic tables in one place. A back forty wouldn't have held them all. They were arranged in neat rows, like headstones in a military graveyard, and each one wore a natty tablecloth of pretty snow. Picnic tables, Bruiser thought. Here where men gnawed at the wasted flesh of starved horses.

He glanced away, down the slope toward distant Misery. Not looking at them, he changed the picnic tables into mud huts, and tried hard to grasp how it must have been, as Lincoln tried to grasp and express how he imagined it had been at nearby Gettysburg. But his postcard imagination betrayed him, and the thought sneaked in through an unguarded flap in the tent: "Boy, this slope sure would make a dandy golf-course fairway."

He closed his eyes and tried to shut that out. He tried to shut out everything but the essentials — the snow, the rocks, the trees; snow and rocks and trees. He tried to isolate himself with the snow and rocks and trees in a way that would put him in touch with the ghosts of the place. Not the ghost of Daddy George, nestled with Martha in the house yonder, but the ghosts of the scruffy sentries who stood guard here on the periphery. He scraped his numb toes on the frozen earth beneath the snow — earth that was a compost of the bloody rags with which those sentries wrapped their rotting feet after their shoes had rotted away.

The dropping sun cast a gold sheen across the snow and spread a soft patina across the distant hilltop trees, and for a moment he thought he might ... It might be possible that ...

But this was just more kidding. He knew that.

Grackles squawked at him from their perch in a nearby gnarled tree, and he scuttled back to the car and pulled on his shoes and socks, looking around sheepishly to see if anyone might have been watching.

The sun set into a tiered conflagration of cloud, and unseen airplanes drew vagrant white lines across the blue twilight, as Bruiser sped away through the rising dusk toward a condition of life that even the redcoats' General Howe, reveling away that other winter in the fleshpots of the colonial capital, could hardly have dreamed, much less that blue-footed sentinel watching the approach of another enemy night with nothing to distract him but the sound of his stomach growling.

CHAPTER TWENTY-FIVE

The Big Dead Rat Campaign

Bruiser's political awareness went back to the whistlestop and A-bomb days of the Truman ascendancy. Politics in the South then was strictly a Democratic Party affair, and the party primary was a midsummer holiday. At twilight on election day, just as the bats and the evening star came out and the clouds purpled away toward evening, his parents would load their brood into Daddy Joe's old pickup and haul them into Sheridan, where the election-night festivities would be getting underway on the courthouse square. The block-square courthouse lawn would be all lit up, decked out with peppermint bunting, and thronged with people from all over Grant County. Little Bruiser would soon lose himself in a Brothers Grimm world of snowcones and redhots, of noisy children running about inventing games while their elders watched the vote totals being chalked up, one precinct at a time through the evening, on a big tote board propped against the speakers' platform. An occasional candidate would glad-hand through the crowd to that platform and regale the attentive, heckled by the screechings of the primitive microphone. Between orators, horrible country singers would torment Orpheus and jug bands would thump and howl. Midnight would pass before enough votes were counted to end the suspense, and by then Little Bruiser would have curled up and gone to sleep on the pallet his mother always brought along, lulled by the democratic racket which was dwarfed into correct perspective by the slow-wheeling constellations overhead.

There was a magic about those nights, and as Bruiser watched the stars and drifted away, he imagined that the political dignitaries, so fluent and incomprehensible, might be emissaries from an enchanted land, from Singapore or Azerbaijan, from Aruba or Capri — from the Land of Politics, where every night must be just such an Arabian night as the one his eyes were closing on. Someday, he thought, he would visit that land, like Marco Polo, and maybe even come to call it his own, like Kubla Khan.

That was no budding ambition; it was only a sleepy child's fleeting fancy. When Little Bruiser was wide awake and not running a fever, he was no more attracted to politics than he was to dentistry or the Detroit Tigers. And during his brief incarnation as a newspaper political writer he saw nothing to tempt him into politics. Indeed, his view of politics darkened during that experience to a shade that would have hauled up Machiavelli. So how could it have come about that during his thirty-third year Bruiser solemnly and publicly announced his intention to seek the vice presidency of the United States? Bruiser wasn't sure himself and deflected the question by quoting Thomas Mann to the effect that modern man cannot understand his destiny in any terms other than political ones, and he said that that despairing thought must have turned his head. Not much of an explanation or excuse, but Bruiser would say no more, and the only other clue to his state of mind at this time is the text of his announcement. Here is what it said:

"I have been called a 'seasoned political observer' for some years now, and my most seasoned political observation is that the vice presidency is the best office that money can buy. It has all the benefits of the presidency with none of the pressures that cause presidents to gutter like candles and wither like prunes. Presidents leave office all pouched and gullied while their veeps go out looking like safari guides. That's no accident. It happens because, while the chief anguishes over the holocaust, the economy and would-be assassins, the veep is out playing golf with Bob Hope or watching the All-Star Game from a choice seat after having thrown out the first ball. The veep gets to travel to interesting places like Korea and Uruguay, all expenses paid, and he doesn't have to wait on his luggage at the airport or stand around the hotel lobby waiting for the maid to finish cleaning his room. He can sit in on the important meetings but isn't obligated to add to the confusion by saying something, and if it gets tedious, nobody minds if he begs pardon and jets off to Key West or Phoenix to lunch with a gang of Wentworths and Graybills, who are always happy to pick up the tab. When the chief is out of town, the veep can sit in the big chair in the Oval Office and nobody chases him out. He can impress his relatives that way, clowning around with the Hot Line; and if any of his old fraternity brothers drop by, he can outprank them by pretending to push the Doomsday button. Also, the money's good."

By coincidence, on the same day that Bruiser made this announcement, and in the same city, Harold Stassen announced that he would be a candidate for the Republican nomination for president. Weird Harold had already run for president more times than Clay and Bryan put together; his battered hat, flung once again into the ring, bore rude heelmarks from four different decades; he was a relic from the days of Tom Dewey and Henry Wallace, an enduring presence, or absence, whom people had long since ceased to pity and now failed even to notice. Could he win the presidency this time? Shorty Fudd wouldn't have given odds, but Bruiser had a hunch. He remembered back in Arkansas an old Quixote named Earnest whose abiding ambition had been to get himself elected county judge. Every election year, Earnest mounted a huge billboard on his pickup, with the hand-painted message: IT'S EARNEST'S TURN. He lost six straight elections using that billboard, and on the seventh try he changed it to read: VOTE FOR EARNEST THIS TIME OR HE QUITS. Folks decided he wasn't kidding and voted him in.

Such a threat might work for Weird Harold, Bruiser thought, particularly since the early competition was proving so weak that No Preference was the early leader in all the polls.

Bruiser assumed he could be Harold's running mate just by offering. Harold was in no position, at least at the start of the campaign, to be choosy; and it wouldn't cost him anything. "False modesty aside," Bruiser told Scamp, "I'd be perfect for the guy. He's from the north and I'm from the south. He's liberal and I can be conservative if that's what he wants. He's old and I'm young. He's a wimp and I'm a lot like Clint Eastwood. He's a lawyer and I'm clean."

"His rug looks like a big rat," Scamp said.

"Aw, that's okay," Bruiser said. "It'll make a good campaign symbol, like the hole in Adlai's shoe. Davy Crockett had his coonskin cap and we'll have our cheap toupee. You see the message it'll convey — Thrifty But With Head Held High."

"What it conveys to me," Scamp said, "is a big dead rat."

Bruiser was anxious to meet with Weird Harold and start plotting the campaign. He sent a telegram to Harold's office: "Accept offer to be your veep. Ready to get started when you are." Harold didn't reply to this wire so Bruiser put in a telephone call to his office. After three rings, a telephone company recording informed him that the number was no longer in service. Bruiser tried, through directory assistance, to find a residential number, but the operator said: "Sorry, I don't show a thing for Statson."

"That's Stassen. S-T-A-S-S-E-N. My God, the man's going to be the next president of the United States."

"Oh, here it is," the operator said, reading him a number which, when he rang it up, turned out to belong to a Harry Stanton.

Bruiser apologized to this Stanton, who was a bouncer at a West Philadelphia strip joint and also the East Coast representative of a Nicaragua firm that manufactured zircon rings. "Yous ever see one of these rings?" he said. "So much like a diamond they'll fool ten percent of your jewelers. Forty dollars, plus tax. Give the little lady a treat, eh?"

"Maybe next time," Bruiser said.

"Passing up the deal of a lifetime, my friend."

"You too," Bruiser said. "You just lost a chance to be the next president of the United States."

"That's okay," Harry said. "I got troubles enough without that."

"I know what you mean," Bruiser said, "but I'd appreciate your vote in November."

"Sure thing," Harry said. "And hey, come by the club sometime. Look but don't touch, you know. Touch one of the girls, your arm's as good as broke, know what I mean?"

"Thanks," Bruiser said.

"Nice talking to yous," Harry said.

Bruiser tried not to be discouraged but the political jockeying was already well underway for the New Hampshire primary and he didn't want to be left at the gate waiting for his nag to show up. It cheered him only slightly to remember Monroe Schwarzlose, the octogenarian turkey farmer back in Arkansas. In Monroe's first race for governor, a public-opinion poll published the day before the election projected that he would run last and attract zero per cent of the vote. Asked to comment, Monroe said: "Well, you don't want your campaign to peak too early, you know."

"That must be Harold's thinking," Bruiser told Scamp. "Lie low here at the start so our campaign won't burn itself out prematurely. Let all these other dopes knock each other off in the early primaries, then we'll slip in and grab the prize. He'll get in touch with me when he gets the strategy worked out."

Scamp rolled her eyes in a fool's-paradise glance at the ceiling, but held her tongue.

The New Hampshire primary came and went, then the Florida primary, and still no word from Harold. It was as though the man had materialized just long enough to toss his hat, and then had returned to the Twilight Zone where he'd lived for a quarter century. Bruiser went so far as to run some classified newspaper ads beseeching and finally daring him to show his face.

When Harold ignored those pleas, too, Bruiser went into a fret. It was too late now to mistletoe himself to another candidate, and it was obvious that Harold didn't intend to exert himself any more in this campaign than he had in the half dozen earlier ones. Bruiser went to the Free Library and scraped the mildew off a couple of old books Harold had written back in the Forties and those books confirmed his worst fears. They revealed Harold to be a man who had outlined a humane and comprehensive political philosophy and who had been waiting ever since for an appreciative nation to beat a path to his door. He would make himself available every four years, but he wouldn't stoop to peddling himself. Bruiser was heartsick. He had yoked himself to an idealist. The pure in heart may be blessed, he knew, but they don't win elections. What could he do now but shoulder the full burden of the Big Dead Rat Campaign himself?

His first task was to raise a warchest. He set a goal of ten million dollars. That was the minimum to draw serious attention to a major political campaign, according to the *New York Times*, which seemed to know what it was talking about. He telephoned his mother back in Arkansas, and she pledged a dollar. He telephoned his brother Bill, who pledged three.

"Four down and just nine million, nine hundred ninety nine thousand, nine hundred ninety six to go," he told Scamp.

Harry Stanton declined an invitation to contribute.

After three days of high-pressure fundraising, Bruiser had amassed cash and pledges amounting to seven dollars and thirty-three cents. He couldn't even sell out to the special interests. Nobody at the National Rifle Association would even talk to him. After he had squandered the entire warchest on a book of stamps and a couple of phone calls, he arranged a consultation with an expert on campaign finance. This expert's name was Steve Lovelady, and he was said to have once worked for, or hung around, or *read* the *Wall Street Journal*.

Lovelady's advice was: "You're not serious?"

"Unfortunately, yes," Bruiser told him.

"Then you don't need financial advice," Lovelady said. "You need medication."

Bruiser persisted and Lovelady said, "All right, the trick is, you don't bleed the moguls by promising them favors. You *scare* money out of them by making them think you'll take away the favors they already have. But you can't scare them unless you convince them you've got a chance to win. In short, you need a campaign treasurer who really knows his stuff, or knows how to rob banks."

"Would you do it?" Bruiser asked.

"Are you kidding?" Lovelady said. "I don't want people laughing at *me*."

Finding a campaign treasurer turned out to be as impossible as finding Harold. Time was a-wasting, meanwhile, and Bruiser had to address an even more urgent matter. Money or no money, the Big Dead Rat Campaign would never get out of the gate unless it let people know what it stood for. Harold had done all he was going to do in that regard in his book *Here I Stand!*, but Bruiser couldn't imagine a political juggernaut fueled by such policies as getting tough with Stalin and bringing back the League of Nations. Bruiser needed to draft an up-to-date platform — he envisioned a series of position papers that would define the Big Dead Rat view on every vital contemporary issue from Abortion to Zionism — but so far during the campaign he hadn't been able to find the time. He realized now that he would have to abandon everything else and take the time.

He was well suited to be the campaign theoretician. He hadn't analyzed the plight of India all those times for nothing. India had ignored him as a podunk editorial writer, but it wouldn't ignore the next vice president of the United States. So on a March evening after supper, Bruiser cloistered himself in the bedroom, got out his writing machine, lit a stogie, rolled up his sleeves, and typed this bold heading on a virgin page:

Big Dead Rat Position Paper # 1
Issue: Abortion

He gave abortion a good thinking about, and was just on the verge of striking a decisive blow either for or against it when Bruiser Jr. dashed in to report with great excitement that Andre the Giant and Haystack Calhoun were tag-teaming two masked heavies in the feature bout on TV. Bruiser Sr.'s view of professional rassling had mellowed; and as a self-proclaimed serious tag-team White House contender, he had come to see the rassling ring as a metaphor for the political arena, and he thought he might learn something from such masters as Andre and Haystack. Fifteen minutes wouldn't make any difference insofar as his manifesto. Abortion would still be there when he got back. Wouldn't Jefferson have taken a break from the Declaration to see the champions of fair play take apart the lardo agents of dirty cheatin' braggadocio?

Abortion was still there, all right, after Bruiser got back to it following the rassling, the NFL game, the late news, Johnny Carson, *Double Indemnity*, the Meditation for Today, and the National Anthem. It was still there the next evening, too. And the next, during which Bruiser decided that it was ten times harder than the agony of India. Maybe twenty times harder.

"How am I supposed to know the instant at which human life begins?" he asked Scamp. "I could make a case for saying it never *has* begun in Tulsa, Oklahoma."

Scamp suggested that he start with something easier and return to abortion after he'd got back into his old issue-espousing groove. So he got out a second paper and, with renewed resolve, typed a heading for it:

Big Dead Rat Position Paper #2
Issue: Balancing the National Budget

This was said to be an important issue in the minds of a great many people. Bruiser wasn't one of those people. He had other mysteries on his mind. Here was one of them:

Once, out of chaos, rock and water converged to form a world. This world spun itself into a big blue ball. Certain elements from the rock and water assumed a quality that would be called life. Those living elements in time developed awareness. This awareness intensified, almost to the point of an independent existence. Almost, but not quite. It continued to be doomed by its dependence on the presence of that quality of life, which came and went, its own existence governed by the whimsical interactions of bits of rock and drops of water. The whole process was constantly stymied, constantly thwarted, constantly *bruised* by the old tag team of paradox and duality. They kept the awareness reeling. They wouldn't let it escape into an understanding of why.

So fish grew lungs and legs and walked and breathed on dry land, dinosaurs foiled extinction by growing wings and becoming hawks, shrews and lemurs contorted themselves into certified public accountants and retired Air Force colonels — and none of them knew why. Some bits of rock and drops of water conjured a living awareness called Bruiser, and Bruiser wanted to know what the hell was going on. But paradox and duality transformed the Bruiser questions into wind. And the Bruiser answers into quicksilver. So the mystery endured, no matter how much Bruiser ranted and raved, no matter how many nights he woke up terrified.

With that weighing on him, Bruiser became annoyed when he considered the possibility that chaos brought forth a blue world, and rocks and water took on the quality of life, and life took on the quality of awareness, and fish walked and dinosaurs flew and simians humanized and humans became conscious of their kinship to parameciums and the stars, for no nobler purpose than a multitude of awareness-endowed mineral water could bandy the issue of whether and how the government of the United States of America might balance its goddam budget.

He obviously wasn't in a frame of mind to compose the second position paper of the Weird Harold Manifesto. The budget, like abortion, would have to season for a time yet.

Big Dead Rat Position Paper #3
Issue: Crime

Scamp noticed that he was espousing his issues (or attempting to) alphabetically — abortion, budget, crime — and alloting each letter only one issue. She wondered if he had a reason for doing it that way.

"Not that I know of," Bruiser said. "I wanted to cover it all from Abortion to Zionism, and if I tried to do all the A's —

agriculture, arms control, atomic stuff — and then all the B's — busing, brinkmanship, bad problems — and all the way through Z, I wouldn't have a manifesto, I'd have a damn encyclopedia."

"What about X?" she said.

"X-rated movies. Not much of an issue, but it lets me use P for something beside porn."

"I got one for E. Endorse the Equal Rights Amendment."

"I'm using E for Energy Policy. The way the A-rabs are gouging us, me and Harold *have* to do a little demagoging on that."

"Arab gouging sounds like A or G to me."

"Well, A's abortion and it looks like G will have to be gasohol."

"Gasowhat?"

"A word that'll soon be on everyone's lips."

"You could use W to endorse the ERA. W for Women's Rights."

"I don't know about that."

"You don't know about what?"

"I'd like to dodge the ERA if I could. I'm not sure I'm ready for it. Personally speaking, I know I couldn't go into a public lounge and use the urinal if a woman was using the one right next to it."

"This isn't something to make stupid jokes about."

"Okay, I'll try to get women's rights in there somewhere."

"Don't do us any favors. Here's the V for you. Vice President Having to Sleep in the Yard."

Scamp was not humorless on this topic, and she knew Bruiser's true sentiments so she wasn't really greatly offended by his oafish teasing, but she was just the tiniest bit put out with him and she affected a slight miff, enough to have him volunteering to wash the supper dishes and clean up the kitchen as penance while she went out to a movie. Scrubbing the casserole pot gave him a chance to contemplate his C issue, Crime, before having to repair to the writing machine to deliver himself on the subject.

Crime: he would be one of how many politicians since the beginning of the world to hustle votes by deploring crime? He estimated five hundred eighty-eight thousand and four. And how many liquor store holdups had been deterred as a result? He estimated nine, suspecting that four was closer to the truth. And at least two of those would have been in some unlikely place like the Sudan.

Turkey, maybe.

He recalled the time when he had been present at an execution. What he remembered most was not the gruesomeness and gore but the way he and the other witnesses and perpetrators avoided looking at one another before, during and after the deed. That wasn't because they thought what they were doing and seeing was wrong, but because they knew it was a testimonial to human failure, a distillation of a general corruption that shrouds human affairs like the mythical ether, a corruption that's a slouching, brutal thing and that commonly expresses itself in the vulgarity of crime and punishment. His task now would be to translate that death-row averting of eyes into political language for the manifesto; translate it into rhetoric, and then into votes, and then into legislation that would essay to remedy something or other. An old sham. Did he really want to be rooting around in such as this?

He got the dishes put away and took out the trash, which included a peck of wadded false starts on a manifesto which would never be written, and which Weird Harold could have told him would never be written, knowing as he did from experience just how far one could indulge the political dream without losing it to that ever looming and circumscribing corruption. He dumped the trash and stood for a moment in the premature late winter darkness that held his Taiwan yard. He remembered lying on his election-night pallet on the Grant County courthouse green and wishing upon the stars — a jasmine vision of politics, faded now to a gray quest for an innocuous sinecure still reeking of Agnew and echoing the jabber of Jubert Jumphrey. Those same stars, a poor child's diamond coverlet, now winked at him like forty-dollar zircons.

CHAPTER TWENTY-SIX

Ideas of the Shipwrecked

Sometimes people in an identity crisis disappear for a time, then turn up again composed, self-confident, and ready to do serious business. That happened with One-Eye, with Zarathustra, with Agatha Christie. With Bruiser, too, who could match insecurities with any of them.

He said of the experience later: "Going off in search of oneself in this fashion is only superficially like a dog chasing its tail. There's no fun in it, for one thing — because when we finally run out of witticisms we get awfully sincere about eternity and all — and while there may be a certain attendant delirium, genuine amnesia is rare, except in the general sense that hardly *any* of us seems to know who we are. The experience can be weird. Scales grew over Saul the tentmaker's eyes and fell off three days later, leaving him a new man. Jesus went forty days in the wilderness without grub, according to Matthew, and 'he was afterward an hungered.' Which sounds right serious to me."

A chase of this sort is always impulsive, if not altogether unexpected, and the descent into crazy isn't necessarily steep. It may start as a whim. So it was that one afternoon after work, Bruiser found himself on the concourse between two trains that were about to depart in opposite directions from Philadelphia. One was the jerky old local that would take him home to his little piece of Taiwan in the suburbs. The other was a smooth, swift express train for New York City. He didn't really decide to board the latter; it just seemed to suck him in and swallow him up. And again he found himself in the gullet of a mechanical beast, hurtling toward some unimaginable rendezvous.

The train ride was a blank, most of it. He paid the conductor for his ticket then promptly dozed off as a way to keep from thinking. When he woke, he still had some sense of time and place and circumstance, but he could feel a great confusion descending.

Disgorged from the train into the great city at dusk, he caught a taxi to the stadium arriving just as one of the first games of the season ended and the crowd came piling through the exits. He went in as they came out, like a sewer rat swimming against the flush, and he spent the night there, in the House That Ruth Built, in a box seat above the home-team dugout. He only had to bribe three different attendants before they agreed to leave him alone.

He slept there — a kind of sleep, anyway, in which a past that never was rose up and rolled by in review exactly as an authentic past would have — and woke in the brown Bronx dawn, one big charleyhorse, with a catbird view of where Yankee Bruiser would have caught fly balls, would have smothered bad-hop grounders, would have fought off the sliders waiting for the hanging curve. Jeez, he might actually have done it. He might actually have been here all those times when he was ... doing what? He tried to be objective about it: the wrists had been good enough, and the eyes, but the arm would have betrayed him and the knees would have been a one-way ticket to Dubuque. He had the heart, though, and could switch-hit, so they might have kept him on as a utility man. But they long since would have traded him to the A's or the Twins, along with cash, for a promising young reliever. He would be finished now, and would know that it had been a mistake, the irretrievable life spent in pursuit of a bouncing ball.

Before the morning was gone, he was on the train again, and it was lapping up Connecticut miles. He tried to nap away his stiffness and the random shooting reminders of his fatigue, but he couldn't rest, and didn't want to rest. New England through the window looked gray and inhospitable, its legacy from the starched pilgrim fathers. It was Saturday now and Boston had left town for the weekend. He paid his respects at the grave of Mother Goose, then caught the silver bullet out to Cambridge, following the cold Bruiser trail into Harvard Yard.

He found a Bruiser graffito or two, but the language was red brick and ivy and he could no longer make sense of it. Was it Authentic Bruiser who had once dozed away the snowy afternoons in his library carrel here among three-hundred-year-old books and called it learning? Or was it the future he was stalking now rather than the past? — would Bruiser Realized, associate professor of uncertainty, be holding forth here at age forty-five? at age sixty? There were tracks in the melting snow — tracks going in, tracks going out again. They led him through Longfellow's yard, but he lost them in the gathering darkness.

He spent the second night in Mount Auburn Cemetery, slumped among the shrubs that surrounded the Greek-oracle tomb of Mary Baker Eddy, prophetess and patron saint of paradox and duality. Her ghost walked that flowered ground, but Bruiser, out of politeness, recalling her insistence that death itself was an illusion and assuming therefore that her ghost wouldn't be able to acknowledge itself, pretended not to see it.

He did get acquainted, though, with cold and hunger during that second night. These weren't the cold and hunger he had burlesqued to conjure at Valley Forge; these were piddling things, like campus radicalism or American sin. They didn't count for much because he was only a thumbride from the depot and a few hours from his old alias and his warm, well-fed ways. He still had a little money in his wallet, so how serious a friend to cold and hunger could he be? But he made their acquaintance as he slept fitfully and raggedly there at the shrine to Mrs. Eddy's muddled dream, and through the night they led him on with hobo rumors of Authentic Bruiser's past or future or maybe even present whereabouts: knocking about Japan with Lafcadio Hearn; gone to Tahiti with Gauguin; to Samoa with Robert Louis Stevenson; to Trieste with Joyce. To Californey with the pioneers, maybe it was; or to the Holy Land with the Crusaders.

It had always filled him with envy and longing and restlessness, they reminded him, when he came across T.E. Lawrence starting a chapter so casually with, "Life in Wejh is interesting," or Conrad in the same offhand way, "One day Heyst turned up in Timor."

Next day Bruiser turned up at the Sleepy Hollow Cemetery at Concord. He followed the Bruiser spoor up the hill, past Emerson's gaudy boulder, to the grave of Thoreau. The initials were so small on the tiny headstone that he could barely make them out, but they were sufficient to imply an inscription: *Simplify.* Bruiser had pondered that inscription when he was here before. It was good advice, but the drift of his life had been toward complication, not simplification. When he should have been subtracting, he had been multiplying by dividing.

Could he start subtracting now?

Days and nights leapfrogged along. He hitchhiked some. He got a little older. He phoned so no one would worry, and reported that he felt like a doomy Robert Frost character, trapped inside the poem and obliged to follow it through to the punchline. He followed the fossilized Bruiser track westward and backward. He didn't see one person in Indiana whose hair wasn't combed. He got as far as Arizona before he felt himself beginning to sink. He felt his sense of purpose slipping away. The saga gradually petered out on him, and the last he could remember he was perched on the lip of the Grand Canyon scared senseless that he was about to fall, or jump, or be swept off into the void by a capricious puff of western breeze.

He closed his eyes and made a wish: All he wanted, Lord, was to be able to open his eyes and find himself in the down-to-earth safety of his own Taiwan bed.

He opened his eyes — and found himself in the down-to-earth safety of his own bed. It was a fact. He couldn't imagine how, but he was back in the familiar hollow of his familiar bed — the successor, four times removed, to that tragic slat-thrower from his honeymoon days. He was back in his bed where he belonged. The house was tranquil with that delicate early-morning stillness, always a surprise, that is one of life's gentle joys. He woke there in that idyll.

He woke enormously relieved but mystified. The sensation was one he supposed he shared with Odysseus, who, on waking that first morning after his return to Ithica, must have wondered if his epic journey had been only a single night's epic dream. Had he really been away? And who had hauled him back, in this time when the gods were reticent and Travis Shellnut was MIA in the vast Asian dreamstate, snatching him from an Apache ledge and transporting him in an instant to the warm hollow of the familiar Bruiser bed? Was it the Bruiser he had been pursuing? Had he caught up with himself for a moment? And what did that foreshadow?

The others soon woke, too, and he discovered that a trip to the shore was scheduled. Before the morning magic had dissipated, he and Scamp and the children were driving east, out of the commonwealth, across the Walt Whitman Bridge, east toward his rendezvous. They missed the turn on to the thoroughfare and soon found themselves negotiating a maze of farm-to-market roads that ran past gray silos and herds of black-and-white dairy cattle, past trim orchards blooming white, past vegetable gardens and plowed fields. It was a slow, smooth landscape, a Breughel, and traversing it unhurriedly, almost destinationless, in the proper company, gave him a sense of making a transition in the proper tempo, which meliorated the vertigo. He found that he was involved in another transition, too, a parallel or concentric one, the occasional scents of manure and sweet clover and running sap causing him to glimpse other Bruisers, phantom hitchhikers, as incorporeal as pavement heat shimmers, whom he had forgotten or never acknowledged. He was making a crossing here, and not just of New Jersey, the Garden State, America's geographical tribute to schizophrenia.

Slowly slowly the landscape transformed, from the doughty inland farms to the freaky pine barrens to the knotty vegetation of the coastal plain. It seemed to him that they might have been on the road forever, or no time at all, when the first seabreeze came up through the car window. The breath of the sea reminded him of the Bruiser who had seen the ocean only once before he was grown but who had always known it in his bones and tears and longing.

Spring hadn't yet arrived at Cape May. The air fanned up over the beach by the breakers still spoke Norse. It would be another week or ten days before the seaside inns and gingerbread hotels marked the onset of the new season by raising their rates and opening their swimming pools. So why had he been drawn here *now*?

It wasn't like before, when he had plunged in among the North Atlantic icebergs. That had been a misunderstanding. He had thought then that the ocean's call was for a reconciliation of estranged chemical elements: that the old rock-and-water, misput since a lunged fish stumped up on to dry land, might find there in ocean's embrace a momentary balance or calm as the blood in his veins and the calcium in his bones commiserated with the seawater, like relatives reminiscing through a wall. Now he knew better. The call was for a reconciliation of estranged elements, all right, but elements of personality rather than chemistry. Time and tide aren't silly, and this wasn't anything as lyrical as seawater calling to an old lost puddle of itself. The summons wasn't into the cold sea, but to the sea's edge.

He wasn't so rash or melodramatic this time. He kept his ears and even his feet dry. He spent the afternoon sitting on the seawall, dodging the ocean spray thrown up from the low-lying rocks and watching optimistic beach fishermen heave their lures in the general direction of France. Prudence. He sat on the seawall watching the children farther down the beach digging in the sand and chasing one another. He watched Scamp lying on a beach towel being worshipped by the lascivious sun.

Clarification, in personality as in moonshine, is achieved by a slow settling.

Nearly a century before, on the opposite side of the world, a man named Paul Claudel had written: "All day long I study the sea as one studies the eyes of a woman who understands. I follow its reflection with the attentiveness of one who listens. In comparison with this pure mirror, how fare the gross intricacies of your tragedies and your ostentations?"

A fair question. So this time he sat on the seawall studying the sea, attentive, considering how the gross intricacies of his tragedies and ostentations fared, waiting for Bruiser.

It was a profitable vigil. He learned something. He learned this: that if Authentic Bruiser came at all, he wouldn't come up from the sea like the birth of Wisdom, or over from the city in a Philadelphia tizzy, or down from Boston or up from Arkansas or gliding in from Arizona. If he came at all, he would converge at seaside from here and there, from past and future, from fact and fancy, from paradox and duality. If that was too cryptic, as someone later said, well, then, too cryptic is how it would have to be.

He was still on the wall when the pure mirror fogged as the continental humidity that had followed him collected like sweat on the brow of the North Atlantic. At twilight, the air became opalescent and diaphanous, hovering over the languid sea in a palpable mixture that he knew would erupt eventually into a Cape May storm.

Faint directionless lightning appeared at midnight, and it must have been an hour later when the first proximate thunderclap shook the fifth-floor hotel balcony where he watched and waited.

The storm went on until after daybreak, the lightning flashes affording spectral fleeting glimpses of the wind-roiled sea.

All the edges had met just right to conjure Bruiser.

After the storm had gone, Bruiser took his family for a walk on the beach. The bottle was in the debris that the stormy surf had left on the wet sand at the water's edge. Bruiser picked it up, and noticed that it had a note in it. The note read:

"This is the simple truth: that to live is to feel oneself lost. He who accepts it has already begun to find himself, to be on firm ground. Instinctively, as do the shipwrecked, he will look around for something to which to cling, and that tragic, ruthless glance, absolutely sincere because it is a question of his salvation, will cause him to bring order into the chaos of his life. The ideas of the shipwrecked are the only genuine ideas. All the rest is rhetoric, posturing, farce. He who does not really feel himself lost is without remission; that is, he never finds himself, never comes up against his own reality."

That message was from a man named Jose Ortega y Gasset, who died on the day that Bruiser donned a Little League uniform and whiffed his way into the legions of the lost. Ortega had lived in a Spanish town that was due east of where Bruiser now stood; and due east of that town was Olympus.

So is the simple truth passed on, in its own good time, perhaps capriciously, perhaps not.

Bruiser put the note back in the bottle, stoppered it tight, and hurled it back into the sea, for time and tide to take it where they would.

CHAPTER TWENTY-SEVEN

On the Hill

It's a Sunday morning in October now, and it's Bruiser's sabbath custom to drive up the hill to the pond at the home place and continue the work that Daddy Joe never finished. The honeysuckle up there never relents in its quest to smother out all the other vegetation, from the blackberry briers to the old oaks, and this morning Bruiser has a machete after some of the most imperialistic clumps. At the same time he has a good fire going in a big pile of the pine limbs that blew down in the most recent windstorm. It's a good day to be out burning: the fall has been unusually rainy, so the pine needles and falling leaves burn with a great deal of aromatic smoke and not much danger of spreading.

Much about the home place is unchanged from the box-turtle days when Bruiser was a barefoot boy here — the same solemn birch trees still stand watch over what Daddy Joe called the jacklot, the same community of crows still disputes every question that comes up in the heavy frowse on the pond's north bank, the algae still threatens to turn the pond into a giant green paramecium. Daddy Joe would surely still recognize his domain. But much about the home place *has* changed, too. It now sports four houses in addition to the clapboard original. These are the homes of two Bucks and two Sisses, and the other three offspring, including Bruiser, live nearby. Another change is that the home place has a trim look about it, in contrast to the days when Daddy Joe littered it with tumbledown outbuildings and with piles of junk that had no discernible purpose but to lacerate the eye while slowly, slowly rusting or rotting away. This tonsured look is mostly the result of the work of Brother Harold and Sister Nita and their bushhogs, but in a different sense it is another generation's different idea of order.

As with the home place, so too with Bruiser. You'll notice, as he drags up an ironwood stump to give some bulk to his fire, that he is much the same but also changed in fundamental ways. He is edging toward fat and graying at the fringe, and he worries that honeysuckle with none of the old dedication and fanaticism. The blows he strikes against it are without malice now; they are blows merely against honeysuckle and not against a metaphor. He knows now, and not just in his head but also in his soul, that the honeysuckle is going to win. And if the struggle against it seems titanic and gargantuan from the inside looking out, he has a notion how important it looks in relief against, say, the Big Bang.

This is not to suggest that Bruiser has mellowed, that he has found some sort of inner peace, that he has some wisdom to share. He has his fishing rod with him, and if the ruminations such as this get too oppressive while he's whacking and burning, he'll tie on a Lucky 13 and take the boat out and amuse the grinnels and kingfishers with a few poorly aimed casts. He's as sorry an excuse for a fisherman as Washington Irving, but after a time he regains his perspective. It won't be the main bout on anybody's card. Probably no one in Rio or Jakarta or Kiev will ever haul up with a pain in the breast and a stifled cry at the thought that once upon a time in a place called Arkansas there existed a unique point of view — a thinking reed, an ambulatory gathering of cells upon which descended, like the Holy Ghost, or more like Casper the Friendly Ghost, really, the identifying Bruiser vapor.

But ah, the grinnel strikes! the primeval bowfin! It doesn't bite the lure as the ordinary bass or bream; it smacks the thing with its tail, flipping it out of the water into the air, where it loops and spins, where it hooks rattle and jingle like a shaman's shaker in that exhilarating and immortal instant before it plops fatly back into the slime.

About the Author

B OB LANCASTER, a winner of the Nieman Fellowship at Harvard, has been a reporter and columnist for the *Philadelphia Inquirer* and three Arkansas newspapers. He is the author of one novel, *Southern Strategy,* and *Judgment Day,* a true-crime account written with B.C. Hall. Now the Senior Editor of the *Arkansas Times* magazine, he lives in his home town of Sheridan, Arkansas.